BLU

Literary Companion

ROME

Compiled by
Annabel Barber

Somerset Books • London

4

Blue Guide Literary Companion Rome
First edition 2011

Published by Blue Guides Limited, a Somerset Books Company
Winchester House, Deane Gate Ave, Taunton, Somerset TA1 2UH
www.blueguides.com
'Blue Guide' is a registered trade mark.

The copyright acknowledgements appearing on p. 304 form a
part of this copyright page. All other in-copyright material
© Blue Guides Limited 2011.

ISBN 978-1-905131-39-6

A CIP catalogue record of this book is available
from the British Library

Distributed in the United States of America by WW Norton and
Company, Inc. of 500 Fifth Avenue, New York, NY 10110

Compiled by Annabel Barber. Grateful thanks are due to
Elizabeth Barber, for much assistance and advice.
Thanks also to Robin Saikia, George Starr and Sophie Willats.
Image research by Hadley Kincade.
Design and typesetting by Anikó Kuzmich,
Annabel Barber, Blue Guides.

Printed and bound in Hungary by Pauker Nyomdaipari Kft.

CONTENTS

Travelling to Rome: An Introduction   7

Mixed Reactions   11

Set Pieces   46

The Colosseum   78

Rome and Religion   96

Papal Rome and St Peter's   130

The Art   160

City of Death   192

Women of Rome   228

Water   249

The Authors   267

General Index   295

Index of Sights   302

Acknowledgements   304

TRAVELLING TO ROME
AN INTRODUCTION

'Diverse pathes leden diverse folk the righte way to Rome.'
Chaucer

'Rome is the great object of our pilgrimage.'
Edward Gibbon

Foreign travellers have always been drawn to Rome, and
they have been 'diverse folk' indeed, from the Christian
pilgrims of the Middle Ages and the Grand Tourists of
the 18th century to the curiosity-seekers of today. Many
of them have written about what they felt, saw and did.
The amount of literature on Rome is prodigious. 'Again
this date of Rome; the most solemn and interesting that
my hand can ever write, and even now more interesting than when I saw it last,' wrote Thomas Arnold to
his wife in 1840. Quoting him in the introduction to
his *Walks in Rome*, Augustus Hare goes on to ask 'how
many thousands before and since have experienced
the same feeling, who have looked forward to a visit
to Rome as one of the great events of their lives, as the
realisation of the dreams and longings of many years?'

A visit to Rome is, or should be, one of the great events
in all travellers' lives. The preparations for a journey can

be elaborate and immense: an Internet search on 'Rome travel guide' yields over five and a half million results, and every literary figure who has ever set foot in the city has consulted a guide of some sort, either in the printed form of a Baedeker or a Murray's Handbook or a Blue Guide, or in the human form of a courier, an antiquary, a *valet de place*—those indispensable accoutrements of the Grand Tourist.

As all literary pilgrims began, so shall we: with a few travel tips. They come from the age of the Grand Tour, written in around 1766 by a certain William Patoun:

William Patoun on arriving in Rome

When your Lordship arrives at Rome, if you have not already secured lodgings, you must bid the postillions carry you to the Hotel de Londres[1] in the Piazza di Spagna, the only inn in Rome. If Barazzi is your banker, by writing to him before you arrive, and acquainting him of the day, he will apply to the Douane, and prevent your Baggage being carried there. I lodged formerly at Rome at a Signor Leoncilli's in the Strada Baboina[2] near the Place d'Espagne. They have very handsome apartments and are good civil people. Lord Ossory lodged there, and before I arrived, the Duke of Grafton, Sir William Stanhope

1 Piazza di Spagna 15. The building has been a bank since 1931.
2 Via del Babuino.

&c...I promis'd to recommend his house: but your Lordship may like some other situation.

A valet de place will be necessary at Rome. They are a most worthless set of scoundrels in general. You must trust to your banker's recommendation.

After you are settled in your lodging and provided with a valet de place, a cicerone is the next necessary *meuble*. There are two young men at Rome at present who act in that capacity. Messrs Morison and Byres[3], both Scotch men and both very worthy...The gratuity given them by any private gentleman is twenty sequins for the course, and thirty if two companions. I need not hint to your Lordship that they are treated on a genteel footing, and have the honour of dining often with all the young men of rank that travel.

The Roman nobility are very civil to strangers of distinction. The families to whom the English commonly have letters are the Borghese, Barberini, Corsini and Giustiniani. The old Princess Borghese is the most sensible woman in Rome and perfectly bred. Her Conversation[4] is every evening, but it is *triste*, and composed of cardinals and abbés. The Princess

---

3 James Byres (1734–1817), a Scottish Jacobite whose family had fled Scotland after the failed rebellion of 1745. An architect and antiquarian, Byres made a career as a guide to Grand Tourists, notably Edward Gibbon.
4 Salon.

Corsini is much at home. [She] is an amiable woman, and of a different cast from most of the Italian ladies. The old Princess Barberini gives the best concerts.

I need not caution your Lordship against purchases at Rome. You have too much taste to buy a bad thing and the good are not to be had. Jenkins, an English picture dealer and broker in the Corso, will try to tempt you. He does not enjoy the best reputation in the world. A certain Major Piccolomini used to haunt the Piazza di Spagna. He pretended to teach fencing by way of favour, but is a notorious sharper… Mr Hamilton the history painter[5] has more true taste then anybody at Rome. He will be very happy to have the honour of attending your Lordship sometimes to the great collections.

From *Advice to a Nobleman*, c.1766

'Methinks I will not die quite happy without having seen something of that Rome of which I have read so much,' wrote Sir Walter Scott. Many shared his views, as the following pages bear witness. The extracts are from commentators both ancient and modern, native and foreign. Short biographical details of each appear at the back of the book.

5 Gavin Hamilton (1723–98), Scottish painter and Jacobite, who settled in Rome in 1756 and worked as an art dealer.

MIXED REACTIONS

'*I don't know why one feels it to be so much superior to other cities—partly the colour I suppose.*'   Virginia Woolf

'*Décidément, je n'aime point Rome.*'   André Gide

Rome exercises great power on the imagination. Epithets such as 'Eternal City' and 'Caput Mundi' endue it with a special portentousness. Travellers planning to go there are caught up in a flurry of anticipation of what they imagine they are going to see and do and feel and become. In past centuries, schoolboys pored over the works of Roman authors: the chance to see the city where those men lived, to walk upon the same stones that their sandals had trodden, was a matter of surpassing excitement. Whoever one was and whatever views, beliefs or prejudices one held, Rome had a claim to be the capital of the world: for Christians, for ardent republicans, for admirers of architecture, for devotees of sculpture, for lovers of sunshine and a 'Latin' lifestyle, for students of law and politics… Carl Jung was so overwhelmed by the idea of what he thought Rome must be that visiting it became impossible for him. Others were so amazed by what they saw—it was so far over and above what they had ever experienced before—that they found they lacked the language to express it, and could only compare it with home.

FIRST IMPRESSIONS

Not many writers, despite their excitement, have allowed themselves to love Rome unconditionally. Most have felt the need to see in it something symbolic, whether of death or eternity or both, but at any rate a microcosmos of the human condition, a lesson to us all. Some authors, refreshingly, permit themselves simply to be delighted. The poet Thomas Gray was one of those. He was twenty-three years old and on the Grand Tour with his schoolfriend Horace Walpole. Edward Gibbon was similarly impressed. He arrived in October 1764 as part of an extended tour of Italy and France. Shelley, too, though he was ambivalent about the city in much of his writing, was impressed by its overall effect.

Thomas Gray is struck dumb

The first entrance of Rome is prodigiously striking. It is by a noble gate, designed by Michel Angelo[1], and adorned with statues; this brings you into a large square, in the midst of which is a vast obelisk of gran-

1 Porta del Popolo.

ite, and at front you have at one view two churches of a handsome architecture, and so much alike that they are called the twins; with three streets, the middlemost of which is the longest in Rome[2]. As high as my expectation was raised, I confess, the magnificence of this city infinitely surpasses it. You cannot pass along a street but you have a view of some palace, or church, or square, or fountain, the most picturesque and noble one can imagine…St Peter's I saw the day after we arrived, and was struck dumb with wonder…

Letter to his mother, 2nd April 1740

Gibbon is intoxicated

My temper is not very susceptible of enthusiasm, and the enthusiasm which I do not feel I have ever scorned to affect. But at the distance of twenty-five years I can neither forget nor express the strong emotions which agitated my mind as I first approached and entered the eternal City. After a sleepless night I trod with a lofty step the ruins of the Forum; each memorable spot where Romulus stood, or Tully[3] spoke, or Caesar fell was at once present to my eye; and several days of intoxication were lost or enjoyed before I could descend to a cool and minute investigation.

From the *Memoirs*, 1796

2 The Corso.
3 Cicero (Marcus Tullius Cicero).

Shelley on looking out across a view of Rome

What shall I say of the modern city? Rome is yet the capital of the world. It is a city of palaces and temples, more glorious than those which any other city contains, and of ruins more glorious than they. Seen from any of the eminences that surround it, it exhibits domes beyond domes, and palaces, and colonnades interminably, even to the horizon; interspersed with patches of desert, and mighty ruins which stand girt by their own desolation, in the midst of the fanes of living religions and the habitations of living men.

Letter to Peacock, 23rd March 1819

Lytton Strachey, friend of Virginia Woolf and member of the Bloomsbury circle, was also delighted by Rome, though when he came to describe it found that he lacked the vocabulary or the experience of anything similar and compared it, rather bizarrely, to Cambridge, another place where he had felt happy and inspired. Other visitors were not so impressed. Horace Walpole, the 'Gothick' novelist, was bored by Rome. He had little to say about the art or the antiquities, and lamented that the social life was dull. 'After sunset one passes one's time here very ill,' he complained, 'the conversations[4] are dreadful things.' Shelley, on closer inspection of individual parts of the city, found himself moralising:

4 *Conversazioni*, evening salons held by Roman ladies.

Shelley on Rome as a symbol of all Italy

In the square of St Peter's there are about three hundred fettered criminals at work, hoeing out the weeds that grow between the stones of the pavement, Their legs are heavily ironed, and some are chained two by two. They sit in long rows, hoeing out the weeds, dressed in parti-coloured clothes. Near them sit or saunter groups of soldiers, armed with loaded muskets. The iron discord of those innumerable chains clanks up into the sonorous air, and produces, contrasted with the musical dashing of the fountains, and the deep azure beauty of the sky, and the magnificence of the architecture around, a conflict of sensations allied to madness. It is the emblem of Italy—moral degradation contrasted with the glory of nature and the arts.

Letter to Peacock, 6th April 1819

Other visitors wanted to find the glory in Rome and did not, and disappointment made them brutal. The English essayist William Hazlitt refused to succumb to the city's charms or to acknowledge any greatness in it, complaining, in language that makes one blush for him, that 'the smell of garlic prevails over the odour of antiquity'. 'This is not the Rome I expected to see,' he moans in his memoirs (1867), and descends into hopeless provincialism to explain why not: 'In Oxford an air of learning breathes from the very walls: halls and colleges meet your eye in every direction; you cannot for a moment forget where you are. In London there is a look of wealth and populousness which is to be found nowhere else. In Rome you are for the most part lost in a mass of tawdry, fulsome common-places…Instead of standing on seven hills, it is situated in a low valley: the golden Tiber is a muddy stream: St Peter's is not equal to St Paul's: the Vatican falls short of the Louvre, as it was in my time[5]; but I thought that here were works immoveable, immortal, inimitable on earth, and lifting the soul half way to heaven. I find them not.'

Wordsworth sees disappointment as salutary

Wordsworth is more philosophical in his disappointment with Rome, as if it can somehow strengthen the soul and lead it to higher things. It was not until later in life that he visited it (he was sixty-seven), by which time he was Wordsworth the Victorian, not Wordsworth the Romantic. The city did not come up to his expectations; for some reason the Capitoline Hill, about which he had read so much, and the Tarpeian Rock, from which the ancients had flung traitors to their deaths, had assumed in his mind the dimensions of Mount Olympus. Yet instead of blaming these things for not being what he had hoped and dreamed, he tried to turn his 'depression' into a force for self-improvement:

5 Hazlitt is being unfair. The Louvre is magnificent in great part because his hero, Napoleon, filled it with booty from his Italian conquests.

At Rome

Is this, ye Gods, the Capitolian Hill?
Yon petty Steep in truth the fearful Rock,
Tarpeian named of yore, and keeping still
That name, a local Phantom proud to mock
The Traveller's expectation?—Could our Will
Destroy the ideal Power within, 'twere done
Thro' what men see and touch,—slaves wandering on,
Impelled by thirst of all but Heaven-taught skill.
Full oft, our wish obtained, deeply we sigh;
Yet not unrecompensed are they who learn,
From that depression raised, to mount on high
With stronger wing, more clearly to discern
Eternal things; and, if need be, defy
Change, with a brow not insolent, though stern.

From *Memorials of a Tour in Italy,* 1837

DIRT & DISSATISFACTION

The squalor of Rome became an obsession with some writers. Tobias Smollett praises the abundant fountains (*see p. 250*) but laments that the water is not put to good use. He was appalled by the filth:

Smollett on Roman dirt

This great plenty of water, nevertheless, has not induced the Romans to be cleanly. Their streets, and even their palaces, are disgraced with filth. The noble Piazza Navona is adorned with three or four fountains, one of which is perhaps the most magnificent in Europe, and all of them discharge vast streams of water: but, notwithstanding this provision, the piazza is almost as dirty as West Smithfield, where the cattle are sold in London. The corridors, arcades, and even staircases of their most elegant palaces, are depositories of nastiness, and indeed in summer smell as strong as spirit of hartshorn. I have a great notion that their ancestors were not much more cleanly. If we consider that the city and suburbs of Rome, in the reign of Claudius, contained about seven millions of inhabitants, a number equal at least to the sum total of all the souls in England; that a great part of ancient Rome was allotted to temples, porticoes, basilicae, theatres, thermae, circi, public and private walks and gardens, where very few, if any, of this great number lodged; that by far the greater part of those inhabitants were slaves and poor people, who did not enjoy the conveniences of life; and that the use of linen was scarce known; we must naturally conclude they were strangely crowded together, and that in general they were a very frowzy generation...When Heliogabalus ordered all the cobwebs of the city and suburbs to be collected, they were found to weigh ten thousand pounds. This was intended as a demonstration of the great number of inhabitants; but it was a proof of their dirt, rather than of their populosity. I might likewise add, the delicate custom of taking vomits at each other's houses, when they were invited to dinner, or supper, that they might prepare their stomachs for gormandising; a beastly proof of their nastiness as well as gluttony. Horace, in his description of the banquet of Nasiedenus, says, when the canopy, under which they sat, fell down, it brought along with it as much dirt as is raised by a hard gale of wind in dry weather.

From *Travels through France and Italy*, 1766

The New York Times on Roman dirt

The City of Rome—Horrible Condition of the Streets
From our own correspondent, Saturday, May 18, 1867
Rome is vile. The goats sleep in it o' nights. You will hardly believe it, but it is the uncolored truth that the streets of the Eternal City, not even excepting the Corso, serve as a stable for thousands of goats that are driven in from the country. They come in late at night, gradually penetrating to the most public streets (the streets of Rome are deserted early), which they also leave earliest in the morning to avoid the stir. They do not leave the quietest alleys till 9 or 10 o'clock. Night and morning you will meet them in long droves. Meantime think of the streets where they slept! Goats eat grass, you know, and a great deal of it. The title of a little pamphlet written by a witty Frenchman ought

to be changed from 'Les odeurs de Rome' to 'Les or-
dures de Rome'.

Dissatisfaction with the annoyances of a big city is by
no means a modern phenomenon. The 1st–2nd-cen-
tury poet Juvenal, in his *Third Satire*, is voluble in his
complaints. Ancient Rome by night was notoriously
noisy. Streets were narrow, not wide enough for one cart
to pass another, and no system of one-way traffic had
been devised. Thus a law was passed that horse-drawn
vehicles were to make their deliveries and do their business after sundown. The din must have been phenom-
enal. Added to this were the attendant dangers. Alberto
Angela evokes it memorably in his *A Day in the Life of
Ancient Rome* (Tr. Gregory Conti, Europa Editions), de-
scribing the night-time streets as 'terrifying as a nocturnal predator', filled with thieves and cut-throats who
had no compunction about knifing the unwary for their
wallet. Ancient Rome, furthermore, had no police force.
Angela may well have been inspired by Juvenal, who
has his own curmudgeonly way of complaining about
the noise and the crowds and the crime:

Juvenal on the problems of urban living

What sleep is possible in a lodging? Who but the
wealthy get sleep in Rome?…The crossing of wagons
in the narrow winding streets, the slanging of drovers
when brought to a stand, would make sleep impos-

sible for a Drusus or a sea-calf![6] When the rich man
has a call of social duty, the mob makes way for him
as he is borne swiftly over their heads in a huge Li-
burnian car[7]. He writes or reads or sleeps inside as
he goes along, for the closed window of the litter in-
duces slumber. Yet he will arrive before us; hurry as
we may, we are blocked by a surging crowd in front,
and by a dense mass of people pressing in on us from
behind: one man digs an elbow into me, another a
hard sedan-pole; one bangs a beam, another a wine-
cask, against my head. My legs are beplastered with
mud; soon huge feet trample on me from every side,
and a soldier plants his hobnails firmly on my toe…

And now regard the different and diverse perils of
the night. See what a height it is to that towering roof
from which a potsherd comes crack upon my head
every time that some broken or leaky vessel is pitched
out of the window! See with what a smash it strikes
and dints the pavement! There's death in every open
window as you pass along at night; you may well be
deemed a fool, improvident of sudden accident, if
you go out to dinner without having made your will.
You can but hope, and put up a piteous prayer in
your heart, that they may be content to pour down

6 A seal. Seals were thought by the Romans to be lazy creatures; Drusus is
obviously a reference that contemporary Romans would have understood.
Scholars are unsure of his identity.
7 Chairmen and litter-bearers traditionally came from Liburnia, a coastal
region in what is now Croatia.

on you the contents of their slop-basins!

Your drunken bully who has by chance not slain his man passes a night of torture like that of Achilles when he bemoaned his friend, lying now upon his face, and now upon his back; he will get no rest in any other way, since some men can only sleep after a brawl. Yet however reckless the fellow may be, however hot with wine and young blood, he gives a wide berth to one whose scarlet cloak and long retinue of attendants, with torches and brass lamps in their hands, bid him keep his distance. But to me, who am wont to be escorted home by the moon, or by the scant light of a candle whose wick I husband with due care, he pays no respect. Hear how the wretched fray begins—if fray it can be called when you do all the thrashing and I get all the blows! The fellow stands up against me, and bids me halt; obey I must. What else can you do when attacked by a madman stronger than yourself?...

Nor are these your only terrors. When your house is shut, when bar and chain have made fast your shop, and all is silent, you will be robbed by a burglar; or perhaps a cut-throat will do for you quickly with cold steel. For whenever the Pontine marshes and the Gallinarian forest[8] are secured by an armed guard, all

8 Two areas of ancient Italy notorious for brigandage and for being difficult to police effectively.

that tribe flocks into Rome as into a fish-preserve.
From the *Third Satire*, late 1st century AD,
Tr. G.G. Ramsay

CONTRASTING IMPRESSIONS

The Victorian poet Arthur Hugh Clough amusingly contrasts two opposed reactions in his poem-in-letters *Amours de Voyage*. The poem is a long one, in effect a novella, and it tells the story of a failed love affair set against a backdrop of war. The date is 1849 and Rome has called upon France to defend her from the armies of Garibaldi, which are fighting to bring an end to papal rule and to unite Italy under a single, national banner. In these early stanzas, though, we see only the reactions of two tourists. Claude is disappointed. He had expected much and finds little. The art and antiquities seem tawdry and pointless; he had left London to experience a foreign land and finds himself spending all his time with his fellow countrymen. (Most 18th- and 19th-century writers remark on this, incidentally: that as soon as an Englishman arrives in Rome, he is descended on by all the other English, calling-cards are left, and visits must be returned.) Clough's other protagonist, Georgina, is charmed with the sights, loving them because she knows she is meant to. The social life, however, she finds a little lacklustre. There are too few English:

I. Claude to Eustace

Dear Eustatio, I write that you may write me an answer,
Or at the least to put us again *en rapport* with each other.
Rome disappoints me much, St Peter's, perhaps, in especial;
Only the Arch of Titus and view from the Lateran please me:
This, however, perhaps is the weather, which truly is horrid.
Greece must be better, surely; and yet I am feeling so spiteful,
That I could travel to Athens, to Delphi, and Troy, and
                                        Mount Sinai,
Though but to see with my eyes that these are vanity also.
Rome disappoints me much; I hardly as yet
                                understand it, but
RUBBISHY seems the word that most exactly would suit it.
All the foolish destructions, and all the sillier savings,
All the incongruous things of past incompatible ages,
Seem to be treasured up here to make fools of present
                                        and future.
Would to Heaven the old Goths had made a cleaner
                                        sweep of it!
Would to Heaven some new ones would come and destroy
                                        these churches!
However, one can live in Rome as also in London.
It is a blessing, no doubt, to be rid, at least for a time, of
All one's friends and relations—yourself (forgive me!)
                                        included—
All the *assujettissement* of having been what one has been,
What one thinks one is, or thinks that others suppose one;
Yet, in despite of all, we turn like fools to the English.

Vernon has been my fate; who is here the same that you
knew him—
Making the tour, it seems, with friends of the name of Trevellyn.

III. Georgina Trevellyn to Louisa ——

At last, dearest Louisa, I take up my pen to address you.
Here we are, you see, with the seven-and-seventy boxes,
Courier, Papa and Mamma, the children, and Mary
and Susan:
Here we all are at Rome, and delighted of course with
St Peter's,
And very pleasantly lodged in the famous Piazza di Spagna.
Rome is a wonderful place, but Mary shall tell you about it;
Not very gay, however; the English are mostly at Naples;
There are the A.'s, we hear, and most of the W party.
George, however, is come; did I tell you about his
mustachios?
Dear, I must really stop, for the carriage, they tell me,
is waiting;
Mary will finish; and Susan is writing, they say, to Sophia.
Adieu, dearest Louise,—evermore your faithful Georgina.
Who can a Mr Claude be whom George has taken to be with?
Very stupid, I think, but George says so VERY clever.....
From *Amours de Voyage*, 1849

A similar contrast of opinion is found in Henry James's *Roderick Hudson*, in the reactions to Rome of the self-satisfied, self-made Mr Leavenworth and the modest

Mary Garland. For the former the past—indeed Europe itself—is of no consequence. For the latter the past becomes something that must be confronted and understood. Here is Leavenworth, regaling us with his chauvinist views while at the same time letting fall to Roderick that the lovely Christina Light is engaged to an Italian prince. The scene takes place in Roderick's studio, where Mr Leavenworth has been admiring a female bust:

Henry James: an American in Rome

'An ideal head, I presume,' [said Leavenworth]; 'a fanciful representation of one of the pagan goddesses—a Diana, a Flora, a naiad or dryad? I often regret that our American artists should not boldly cast off that extinct nomenclature.'

'She is neither a naiad nor a dryad,' said Roderick, 'and her name is as good as yours or mine.'

'You call her'—Mr Leavenworth blandly inquired.

'Miss Light,' Rowland interposed, in charity.

'Ah, our great American beauty! Not a pagan goddess—an American, Christian lady! Yes, I have had the pleasure of conversing with Miss Light. Her conversational powers are not remarkable, but her beauty is of a high order. I observed her the other evening at a large party, where some of the proudest members of the European aristocracy were present—duchesses, princesses, countesses, and others distinguished by similar titles. But for beauty, grace, and elegance my fair countrywoman left them all nowhere. What women can compare with a truly refined American lady? The duchesses the other night had no attractions for my eyes; they looked coarse and sensual! It seemed to me that the tyranny of class distinctions must indeed be terrible when such countenances could inspire admiration. You see more beautiful girls in an hour on Broadway than in the whole tour of Europe. Miss Light, now, on Broadway, would excite no particular remark.'

'She has never been there!' cried Roderick, triumphantly.

'I'm afraid she never will be there. I suppose you have heard the news about her.'

'What news?' Roderick had stood with his back turned…but at Mr Leavenworth's last words he faced quickly about.

'It's the news of the hour, I believe. Miss Light is admired by the highest people here. They tacitly recognise her superiority. She has had offers of marriage from various great lords. I was extremely happy to learn this circumstance, and to know that they all had been left sighing. She has not been dazzled by their titles and their gilded coronets. She has judged them simply as men, and found them wanting. One of them, however, a young Neapolitan prince, I believe, has after a long probation succeeded in making himself acceptable. Miss Light has at last said yes, and the engagement has just been announced. I am not generally a retailer of gossip of this description, but the fact was alluded to an hour ago by a lady with whom I was conversing, and here, in Europe, these conversational trifles usurp the lion's share of one's attention. I therefore retained the circumstance. Yes, I regret that Miss Light should marry one of these used-up foreigners. Americans should stand by each other. If she wanted a brilliant match we could have fixed it for her. If she wanted a fine fellow—a fine, sharp, enterprising modern man—I would have undertaken to find him for her without going out of the city of New York. And if she wanted a big fortune, I would have found her twenty that she would have had hard work to spend: money down—not tied up in fever-stricken lands and worm-eaten villas! What is the name of the young man? Prince Castaway, or some such thing!'

It was well for Mr Leavenworth that he was a voluminous and imperturbable talker; for the current of his eloquence floated him past the short, sharp, startled cry with which Roderick greeted his 'conversational trifle'. The young man stood looking at him with parted lips and an excited eye...

From *Roderick Hudson*, 1875

These opinions of Mr Leavenworth are contrasted later with those of Mary Garland, Roderick's fiancée, with whom Roderick's friend Rowland is secretly in love. Her provincial American background (she is from a simple family of pastors) has taught her nothing of art or the Classical world, but she has read widely. She comes to Rome with an open mind, saying, confidently, 'I expect to enjoy it.' Enjoyment, though, for her, is allied to trouble. For to enjoy Rome to the full, she has to adapt herself to its pulse. Here they are on a trip to St Peter's:

Henry James: a very different American in Rome

From the moment the carriage left the hotel, [Miss Garland] sat gazing, wide-eyed and absorbed, at the objects about them. If Rowland had felt disposed he might have made a joke of her intense seriousness. From time to time he told her the name of a place or a building, and she nodded, without looking at him. When they emerged into the great square between Bernini's colonnades, she laid her hand on Mrs Hudson's arm and sank back in the carriage, staring up at the vast yellow façade of the church. Inside the church, Roderick gave his arm to his mother, and Rowland constituted himself the especial guide of Miss Garland. He walked with her slowly everywhere, and made the entire circuit, telling her all he knew of the history of the building. This was a great deal, but she listened attentively, keeping her eyes fixed on the dome. To Rowland himself it had never seemed so radiantly sublime as at these moments; he felt almost as if he had contrived it himself and had a right to be proud of it. He left Miss Garland a while on the steps of the choir, where she had seated herself to rest, and went to join their companions. Mrs Hudson was watching a great circle of tattered *contadini*[9], who were kneeling before the image of St Peter. The fashion of their tatters fascinated her; she stood gazing at them in a sort of terrified pity, and could not be induced to look at anything else. Rowland went back to Miss Garland and sat down beside her.

'Well, what do you think of Europe?' he asked, smiling.

'I think it's horrible!' she said abruptly.

'Horrible?'

'I feel so strangely—I could almost cry.'

'How is it that you feel?'

'So sorry for the poor past, that seems to have died here, in my heart, in an hour!'

'But, surely, you're pleased—you're interested.'

'I am overwhelmed. Here in a single hour, everything is changed. It is as if a wall in my mind had been knocked down at a stroke. Before me lies an immense new world, and it makes the old one, the poor little narrow, familiar one I have always known, seem pitiful.'

'But you didn't come to Rome to keep your eyes fastened on that narrow little world. Forget it, turn

9 Country people, peasants.

your back on it, and enjoy all this.'

'I want to enjoy it; but as I sat here just now, look-ing up at that golden mist in the dome, I seemed to see in it the vague shapes of certain people and things at home. To enjoy, as you say, as these things demand of one to enjoy them, is to break with one's past. And breaking is a pain!'

'Don't mind the pain, and it will cease to trouble you. Enjoy, enjoy; it is your duty…'

She looked away from him for some moments, down the gorgeous vista of the great church. 'But what you say,' she said at last, 'means change!'

From *Roderick Hudson*, 1875

ROME AS A FORCE FOR CHANGE

The purpose of travel, or one of them, is to see new things and learn from them. Very often these lessons reveal new aspects of our own selves—and the falling scales have provoked much voluble writing. One of the foreigners who most famously found inspiration in Rome, and who did feel—to use Mary Garland's im-age—that a wall in his mind had been knocked down, bringing with it new vistas, a discovery of self, which shaped his future development, both personal and ar-tistic, was Goethe. For many foreigners, Rome, and in-deed Italy in general, represented freedom, which in the

worst cases translated into a license to behave badly, far
from the moral strictures of home and in a milieu where
no one knew who you were or would care what you
did. Away from one's own people, one is judged differ-
ently, and is not expected to conform to local moralities.
There is nothing to suggest that Goethe behaved particularly badly. But Rome for him was both a revelation
and a revolution, a grand awakening of the soul and
the senses. Italy exercised a great formative influence
on him; his *Italian Journey* expresses his delight at seeing lemon trees for the first time, at seeing the sea, at
feeling his senses (as so many northerners have) come
alive in a kinder climate. The reflection of this personal
Renaissance can be seen in his poetry. Suddenly his
verse is strewn with Classical allusions and paeans to
pagan deities. Erotically, too, Italy was a milestone in
Goethe's life. He does not say as much in his memoirs,
but his *Roman Elegies* speak for themselves. In perhaps
the most famous of these he describes how he learns
to appreciate sculpture by caressing the forms of his
lover's body, and how physical love inspires him to poetry. Once his mistress has fallen asleep in his arms, he
lies awake composing, counting out the hexameters on
her naked back. In the Elegy quoted here he contrasts
brilliant Rome with the murky north he has left behind
him. Rid of his stultifying job and having run away from
a love affair that was intellectual instead of physical, he
portrays himself as an aspirant votary at Jupiter's shrine:

Goethe is a changed man

Oh, how happy I feel here in Rome! To think of
                                        that past life
When in the chill, clammy north grey days and fog
                                        clung about me,
Heavy and lowering skies pressed themselves down
                                        on my head.
All that I knew was fatigue, a formless and
                                        monochrome world,
Thus I turned on myself, sank deep into contemplation,
    Scanning the murky paths of my discontented soul.
Now, though, my brow is aglow; radiant air shines upon it;
    Bright Apollo makes summons, calls colours and
                                        shapes into life.
Star-bright glimmers the night, it hums with tender singing,
    And more brilliant the moon, brighter than northern sun.
Oh, what blessings upon my mortality! Do I dream?
                                        Does truly
    Thy ambrosial house receive me, Jove, as a guest?
Ah! Recumbent I stretch both my hands to thy knees,
    In supplication, O Jove, Jupiter Xenius[10], receive me!
How I came in here I know not, save that the
                                        beautiful Hebe
    Seized the pilgrim and drew him willingly into these halls.
Hadst thou demanded a hero be brought to thy
                                        godly abode?

10 Jupiter the Hospitable.

Forgive her, then, if she mistook! But let me gain
                                                                 much by the error!
Your daughter Fortuna is also—so girlish in habit—
    Bestowing the choicest of gifts, purely according to whim!
Art thou the hospitable god? Oh then, do not
                                                                 banish thy guest,
    Nor cast him out of Olympus back down to
                                                                 earth once again!
'Poet! To where art thou climbing?'—Forgive me; the lofty
    Hill of the Capitol is truly thy second abode.
Suffer me, Jove, to remain, and later Hermes will lead me
    Past old Cestius' mound[11], softly to Hades below.

                                        Roman Elegy no. 7, 1795 (Tr. AB)

Another portrait of Rome's power to change the course
of lives and destinies comes from George Eliot's novel
Middlemarch. The young Dorothea, who has confound-
ed family expectations by marrying Edward Casaubon,
an earnest scholar several years her senior, is in Rome
on her honeymoon. Her husband is writing a magnum
opus entitled *The Key to All Mythologies*. Dorothea is
keen to aid him with this great task, but he shows little keenness to involve her. Indeed, he has warned her
that 'You will have many lonely hours, Dorothea, for I
shall be constrained to make the utmost use of my time

---

11 The Pyramid of Gaius Cestius, behind which lies the Protestant Cemetery. By a twist of fate, Goethe's only son is buried there.

during our stay in Rome', by which he means studying manuscripts in the Vatican Library. The experience in Rome is a turning-point for them both.

George Eliot on Rome and self-knowledge

Dorothea had now been five weeks in Rome, and in the kindly mornings when autumn and winter seemed to go hand in hand like a happy aged couple one of whom would presently survive in chiller loneliness, she had driven about at first with Mr Casaubon, but of late chiefly with Tantripp and their experienced courier. She had been led through the best galleries, had been taken to the chief points of view, had been shown the grandest ruins and the most glorious churches, and she had ended by oftenest choosing to drive out to the Campagna where she could feel alone with the earth and sky, away from the oppressive masquerade of ages, in which her own life too seemed to become a masque with enigmatical costumes.

To those who have looked at Rome with the quickening power of a knowledge which breathes a growing soul into all historic shapes, and traces out the suppressed transitions which unite all contrasts, Rome may still be the spiritual centre and interpreter of the world. But let them conceive one more historical contrast: the gigantic broken revelations of that Imperial and Papal city thrust abruptly on the notions of a girl who had been brought up in English and Swiss Puri-

tanism, fed on meagre Protestant histories and on art
chiefly of the hand-screen sort; a girl whose ardent nature turned all her small allowance of knowledge into
principles, fusing her actions into their mould, and
whose quick emotions gave the most abstract things
the quality of a pleasure or a pain; a girl who had lately
become a wife, and from the enthusiastic acceptance
of untried duty found herself plunged in tumultuous
preoccupation with her personal lot. The weight of
unintelligible Rome might lie easily on bright nymphs
to whom it formed a background for the brilliant pic-
nic of Anglo-foreign society; but Dorothea had no
such defence against deep impressions…

Dorothea was crying…, for that new real future
which was replacing the imaginary drew its material from the endless minutiae by which her view of
Mr Casaubon and her wifely relation, now that she
was married to him, was gradually changing with
the secret motion of a watch-hand from what it had
been in her maiden dream…Since they had been in
Rome, with all the depths of her emotion roused to
tumultuous activity, and with life made a new problem by new elements, she had been becoming more
and more aware, with a certain terror, that her mind
was continually sliding into inward fits of anger and
repulsion, or else into forlorn weariness…

When [Mr Casaubon] said, 'Does this interest you,
Dorothea? Shall we stay a little longer? I am ready

to stay if you wish it,'—it seemed to her as if going or staying were alike dreary. Or, 'Should you like to go to the Farnesina, Dorothea? It contains celebrated frescoes designed or painted by Raphael, which most persons think it worth while to visit.'

'But do you care about them?' was always Dorothea's question.

'They are, I believe, highly esteemed. Some of them represent the fable of Cupid and Psyche, which is probably the romantic invention of a literary period, and cannot, I think, be reckoned as a genuine mythical product. But if you like these wall-paintings we can easily drive thither; and you will then, I think, have seen the chief works of Raphael, any of which it were a pity to omit in a visit to Rome. He is the painter who has been held to combine the most complete grace of form with sublimity of expression. Such at least I have gathered to be the opinion of cognoscenti.'

This kind of answer given in a measured official tone, as of a clergyman reading according to the rubric, did not help to justify the glories of the Eternal City, or to give her the hope that if she knew more about them the world would be joyously illuminated for her.   From *Middlemarch*, 1874

The capacity of Rome to show us the world in a different light is a theme taken up by Madame de Staël. In her romantic novel of 1807, entitled *Corinne, ou l'Italie*, she idealises and idolises the character of the Italian people, a character which she defines as simple, warm, affectionate, sincere, naturally poetic—embodying all the virtues, in fact, that a person who had admired Rousseau and his noble savage (as de Staël had fervently done) would wish to attribute to an ideal race.

Corinne, the mysterious poetess and artist, becomes the muse and instructress of the melancholy Scotsman Oswald, Lord Nelvil, who meets her in Rome. Together they set out to 'discover' Italy—and on the journey, of course, Lord Nelvil discovers love. What he does not discover is that he and Corinne have a history in common. In this extract Lord Nelvil sees Corinne for the first time as she arrives at the Capitoline Hill to be crowned Poet Laureate, as Petrarch had been before her:

Madame de Staël on Rome's inspiring power

Oswald wandered the streets of Rome, awaiting the appearance of Corinne. At every turn he heard her spoken of, learned of some new quality in her which suggested a confluence of all those talents which can capture the imagination. Her voice, said one, was the most affecting in Italy; another claimed that none could play tragedy like she; still another that she danced like a nymph and that she sketched with as much artistry as invention. All were agreed that none had ever composed or extemporised such lovely verse, and that in her daily intercourse she exhibited a grace and eloquence that charmed everyone. It was disputed which town in Italy had given her birth; but the Romans boldly averred that she must have been born at Rome to speak so pure an Italian. The name of her family was unknown. Her first work had appeared five years before and had given as its author simply 'Corinne'. No one knew where she had lived, nor even what her life had been before now. She was at this time about six and twenty. Such mystery allied to such publicity, a woman of whom all the world was talking and yet whose true name was unknown, seemed to Lord Nelvil one of the marvels of this singular country he had journeyed so far to see. In England he would have judged such a woman very harshly, but he applied none of the customary social conventions to Italy, and the crowning of Corinne inspired, in anticipation, an interest such as might have been produced by a tale of Ariosto.

A beautiful, stirring music announced the arrival of the triumphal procession. Any event, whatever its nature, that is heralded by music, must needs be productive of emotion. A multitude of Roman lords, mingled with some strangers, preceded Corinne's chariot. 'It is her cortège of admirers,' said one Roman. 'Yes,' said another, 'All the world pays tribute to her, but she accords no special preference to anyone. She is rich, independent. It is even said—and certainly she has that look about her—that she is a woman of high birth who does not wish to be known.'

'Whatever the truth,' said a third, 'she is a goddess environed by clouds.'

Oswald looked at the man who had thus spoken, and everything about him designated him a person of the meanest degree; but in the South one is formed by nature to use expressions so poetic that one may suppose them engendered on the air and begotten by the sun.

At length the four white horses drawing Corinne's car began to make their way through the crowd. Corinne was seated on this conveyance, which was constructed after the antique manner, and beside it walked a procession of young maidens dressed in white. As Corinne passed, the crowd flung incense in the air. Everyone had turned out at their windows to see her and the casements were held wide by vases of flowers and scarlet rugs. Loud were the acclamations: 'Long live Corinne! Long live genius! Long live beauty!' The emotion was general, but Lord Nelvil did not share in it as yet, and though he had already reminded himself that, to judge all this, he must put aside all English reserve and French levity, he was unable to give himself up to this festival—until the moment when he espied Corinne.

She was costumed as a Sibyl, a shawl of India muslin wound around her head, and tresses of the purest black entwined with the shawl. Her gown was white,

with a blue sash attached below her breast: her dress
was very picturesque, without, however, departing so
far from accustomed usage as to speak of affectation.
Her deportment on the car was noble and modest…
she gave at once the idea of a priestess of Apollo, advancing toward the temple of the Sun.

From *Corinne, ou l'Italie*, 1807 (Tr. AB)

ROME WITHOUT ITALIANS

'Rome is certainly the only city in which a stranger
without family or acquaintance can settle and be, as
it were, at home.' So said Hans Christian Andersen in
1842. Not many other visitors have felt the same. Un-
derpinning a large number of the writings on Rome
is a sense of escapism, of wanting to get away and to
project onto the unfamiliar environment one's ideal of
what should be. Travellers have frequently found what
they wanted to find, and seen in a people whom they
do not fully know or understand a kind of prelapsarian
ideal, born of dissatisfaction with home, of the quest
for sunshine and the lure of some kind of nameless
romance. Others simply see a ruffianly race, a confir-
mation of their own sense of national superiority. The
18th-century author and playwright Oliver Goldsmith
was optimistic to claim that foreign travel would be
beneficial for 'the shaking off of national prejudices,

and the finding nothing ridiculous in national peculi-
arities'. Many writers who came to Rome were certainly
not thus edified, and left with their prejudices completely intact. The English, in any case, were famous
for sticking together. And even those travellers who did
meet Romans often failed signally to befriend or understand them, or even to find them interesting. One
was always shielded by one's courier, whose role, as
Ruskin candidly remarks, was to 'save the family unbe-
coming cares and mean anxieties, besides the trouble
and disgrace of trying to speak [a] foreign language.'
Claire Clairmont, former lover of Lord Byron, writes
the following in her journal in 1819: 'In the Evening
go to the Conversazione[12] of the Signora Marianna Di-
onigi, where there is a Cardinal and many unfortunate
Englishmen, who after having crossed their legs and
said nothing the whole evening, rose up all at once,
made their bows and filed off.' This state of affairs, ap-
parently, was not new. In 1766 William Patoun had
warned that 'The conversationi are the dullest things
in the world. You go in, you make your bow to the
lady of the house, you stare at the company playing at
games for sixpences which you never are at the pains
to learn and then you huddle with the groups of English into a corner, talk loud, often at the expense of the
company, grow tired and go home.'

12 Salon.

One of the very finest expressions of the phenomenon of people visiting Rome to escape, to create the world they want in an environment in which they have no stake and feel no responsibility, comes from an Italian, Carlo Levi, in an essay entitled 'Sunday Stroll'. Levi is walking in the Borghese Gardens, and comes upon a puppet show, which ends with a thrice-repeated sequence of Punchinello coming face to face with death:

Carlo Levi on Rome without Italians

Even the children seemed a little frightened. They, who always know by heart every line and every move of this their own theatre and who defend every aspect against change, were bemused by this story of devils, death, and perhaps psychoanalysis, resembling a scene from the Mexican 'Day of the Dead' ritual. Or perhaps, in the happy dreamy Sunday atmosphere, this was nothing but a reminiscence of the baroque era and the Counter-Reformation, an image from Belli[13], dropped artfully before its proper audience: nannies, soldiers, and children.

That men, whether living or dead,
Have a death's head within their own head.

What sort of death's head the American woman at the counter of the café concealed in her beautifully

---

13 The popular Roman poet Gioacchino Belli (1791–1863).

groomed head, a few steps further along, was not easy to say. It was hard to say how old she might be, somewhere between fifty, perhaps, and seventy, exceedingly elegant, made-up, clearly an adept of massages, beauty treatments, creams, and science. Her hair was dyed white, with the slightest haze of light blue; her unwrinkled face was daubed girlishly in pink, her tiny hands emerged from long, well-made black suede gloves, her petite feet were enclosed in exceedingly soft slippers adorned with a silk bow, her black silk outfit was studded with ornaments and decorated with frills, at once sober and fanciful. She was an elegant 'sophisticate' from Park Avenue, and at that time of day she wore her drunkenness with confident stylishness. She spoke English to the barman, and he answered in the same language. She was drinking a negroni.

'Can I take a bottle of negroni *originale* back with me to America?'

'Of course.'

'How do you make it?'

'One part bitters, one part Carpano, and the rest gin.'

'No, no gin.'

Without gin, it's not a negroni; it's something else.'

'But I want a negroni *originale* without gin.'

With her negroni she was eating buttered canapés with caviar and salmon.

'Why are they buttered?'

'That's how we make them here: they are buttered canapés.'

'Couldn't I have them without butter?'

'Sure, but then they would be something different. The Italians like their canapés buttered.'

'Couldn't I have Rome without the Italians?'

Negroni without gin, canapés without butter, Rome without Italians; this scene out of Hemingway went on and on, starting all over again for pages and pages: Rome, the canapés, the negronis, the negronis, the canapés and Rome, and so on. There were no bulls, no bullfighters awaiting us. Only, if I had chosen, the canvases of the so-called 'Giovane pittura' (*giovane* referring to the youthful ages of the artists themselves) in Valle Giulia, where I was now walking, just as arid, elegant, and empty as the youthful soul of the elderly American woman.

From *Fleeting Rome: In Search of La Dolce Vita*,
Tr. Antony Shugaar

SET PIECES

One does not have to read very many of the novels and travelogues of past centuries to realise that there was a clear itinerary for visitors to Rome. Certain things were on their map; others are seldom mentioned. It is much the same today, where all guide books concentrate on the same things: the menu has changed little from the days of Murray and Baedeker, and indeed it was established long before that by the couriers and antiquarians who took the young milords around town. The Forum was always visited, as were the Colosseum, St Peter's, the catacombs, the Spanish Steps and Piazza di Spagna. Though not a tourist attraction in the same way, the Jewish ghetto was also sought out by many.

THE FORUM

If early writers are relatively silent about the Forum, it is because it remained unexcavated until the later part of the 19th century (excavations in fact continued well into the 20th century and are still taking place today). Before this the Forum was an area of pastureland, known as the Campo Vaccino, where people would turn their cattle loose to graze among the column stumps. One gets a fair impression of it from the engravings of Piranesi, and many writers found its desolation romantic. As Shelley described it in 1819, 'The ruins of the ancient Forum are so far fortunate that they have not been walled up in the modern city. They stand in an open, lonesome place, bounded on one side by the modern city, and the other by the Palatine Mount, covered with shapeless masses of ruin.' The American writer W.D. Howells was impervious to any romance. 'In hollows below the level of the dirty cowfield,' he wrote in 1867, 'wandered over by evil-eyed buffaloes, and obscenely defiled by wild beasts of men, there stood here an arch, there a pillar, yonder a cluster of columns crowned by a bit of frieze; and yonder again, a fragment of temple, half-gorged by the façade of a hideous Rococo church.'

Elizabeth Bowen, in *A Time in Rome* (written after excavation had taken place, by which time many of the churches that so offended Howells had been removed) devotes several pages to the Forum, attempting to conjure up what it would have been like in ancient times, when it was the civic and religious centre of the city:

Elizabeth Bowen on the Forum

All said and done, why re-evoke the Forum?—why should my senses wish to do so? As it was, it would have been insupportable: heatedness, glare, clamour beating like so many gongs on the brain. When the overhanging buildings, all day sunstruck, sent up a quiver dulled by ascending dust to a copper haze; or when wind howled through the porticoes, having to be out-shouted, whipping rain aslant into foul brown puddles—who could wish to be there? Tension wired the air of this hemmed-in valley, by physical nature torpid, staled by sweat, exhausted by lungs. And to the overcrowding, surging and shoving living and breathing humans on the outdoor floor was added a population of statues, at every eminence—topping columns, looking out in rows from the arcaded windows of upper storeys, or lined up along the parapets of roofs. Some gesticulated, others struck athletic or martial attitudes, others, arms folded, remained in a blind sternness of which the meaning must have worn off. Over that theatre of the mortal passions these stood for the only immortality to be hoped for. Nor were they all: on the tops of arches for ever pranced teams of ferocious horses; others snorted beneath Imperial riders. To human and animal agitation was added a flapping of gilded wings by sub-divinities and extended eagles. High points of bronze, gilded bronze, or actual gold shot forth ostentatious rays where the sun caught them, among the glossy monotony of marbles. Work on one building if not another being almost continually in progress, there can seldom not have been scaffolding in the Forum, together with heaving, hauling, and hammering...

From *A Time in Rome*, 1959

Quo Vadis, by the Polish Nobel-prizewinning author Henryk Sienkiewicz, is a historical novel set in the time of Nero. It follows the fortunes of a young Christian woman, Lygia, and her Roman lover, Marcus Vinicius, nephew of the stylish, world-weary Petronius Arbiter, Nero's umpire on taste and aesthetics. After the city of Rome burns in a terrible fire (*see p. 111*), Nero seeks to veil his own incompetent handling of the crisis by launching a pogrom against the Christian population. We take up the story near the beginning: Vinicius has told his uncle that he has met an extraordinary woman and fallen in love with her. The two decide to visit her at the house of Aulus Plautius, where she lives as the family's adopted daughter (she is in fact a barbarian from an area now covered by modern Poland):

Henryk Sienkiewicz on the Forum

The litter was waiting long since; hence they took their places, and Petronius gave command to bear them to the Vicus Patricius, to the house of Aulus. Petronius' 'insula' lay on the southern slope of the Palatine, near the so-called Carinae; their nearest way, therefore, was below the Forum; but since Petronius wished to step in on the way to see the jeweller Idomeneus, he gave the direction to carry them along the Vicus Apollinis and the Forum in the direction of the Vicus Sceleratus, on the corner of which were many tabernae of every kind.

Gigantic Africans bore the litter and moved on, preceded by slaves called *pedisequii*. Petronius, after some time, raised to his nostrils in silence his palm odorous with verbena...From the Vicus Apollinis they turned to the Boarium, and then entered the Forum Romanum, where on clear days, before sunset, crowds of idle people assembled to stroll among the columns, to tell and hear news, to see noted people borne past in litters, and finally to look in at the jewellery shops, the bookshops, the arches where coin was changed, shops for silk, bronze, and all other articles with which the buildings covering that part of the market placed opposite the Capitol were filled.

One half of the Forum, immediately under the rock of the Capitol, was buried already in shade; but the columns of the temples, placed higher, seemed golden in the sunshine and the blue. Those lying lower cast lengthened shadows on marble slabs. The place was so filled with columns everywhere that the eye was lost in them as in a forest...Above that forest gleamed coloured triglyphs; from tympans stood forth the sculptured forms of gods; from the summits winged golden quadrigae seemed ready to fly away through space into the blue dome, fixed serenely above that crowded place of temples. Through the middle of the market and along the edges of it flowed a river of people; crowds passed under the arches of the basilica of Julius Caesar; crowds were sitting on the steps of Castor and Pollux, or walking around the temple of Vesta, resembling on that great marble background many-coloured swarms of butterflies or beetles. Down immense steps, from the side of the temple on the Capitol dedicated to Jupiter Optimus Maximus, came new waves; at the rostra[1] people listened to chance orators; in one place and another rose the shouts of hawkers selling fruit, wine, or water mixed with fig-juice; of tricksters; of vendors of marvellous medicines; of soothsayers; of discoverers of hidden treasures; of interpreters of dreams…From time to time the crowds opened before litters in which were visible the affected faces of women, or the heads of senators and knights, with features, as it were, rigid and exhausted from living. The many-tongued population repeated aloud their names, with the addition of some term of praise or ridicule. Among the unordered groups pushed from time to time, advancing with measured tread, parties of soldiers, or watchers, preserving order on the streets. Around about, the Greek language was heard as often as Latin.

Vinicius, who had not been in the city for a long time, looked with a certain curiosity on that swarm of people and on that Forum Romanum, which both dominated the sea of the world and was flooded by

---

1 The speakers' tribunes, decorated with *rostra*, the prow-rams of captured ships.

it, so that Petronius, who divined the thoughts of his companion, called it 'the nest of the Quirites—without the Quirites[2].' In truth, the local element was well-nigh lost in that crowd, composed of all races and nations. There appeared Ethiopians, gigantic light-haired people from the distant north, Britons, Gauls, Germans, sloping-eyed dwellers of Lericum; people from the Euphrates and from the Indus, with beards dyed brick colour; Syrians from the banks of the Orontes, with black and mild eyes; dwellers in the deserts of Arabia, dried up as a bone; Jews... Egyptians...Numidians and Africans; Greeks from Hellas...Greeks from the islands, from Asia Minor, from Egypt, from Italy, from Narbonic Gaul...There were priests of Serapis, with palm branches in their hands; priests of Isis, to whose altar more offerings were brought than to the temple of the Capitoline Jove; priests of Cybele, bearing in their hands golden ears of rice; and priests of nomad divinities; and dancers of the East with bright head-dresses, and dealers in amulets, and snake-tamers, and Chaldean seers; and, finally, people without any occupation whatever, who applied for grain every week at the storehouses on the Tiber...

> From *Quo Vadis: A Narrative of the Time of Nero*, 1896, Tr. Jeremiah Curtin

2 Roman citizens.

THE GHETTO

In 1556 Pope Paul IV commanded that the Jews of Rome should live segregated in the Ghetto, an area beside the Tiber bank on the site of an ancient circus. The Ghetto walls were pulled down in 1848; in 1943 over two thousand Roman Jews were deported to concentration camps. Many Jews still live in the old Ghetto area, which is filled with shops selling kosher produce and Judaica, and with restaurants serving Roman Jewish cuisine.

When Benjamin of Tudela visited the city, some time in the later part of the 12th century, he found Roman Jewry in a good state and on amicable terms with the papacy—at that time they were not confined to a ghetto and restrictions had not been placed on their freedom. Five hundred years later John Evelyn visited the Ghetto, on the invitation of a friend, and in his diary left a fascinating account of a circumcision. William Hazlitt, in 1826, was scathing about the condition of the Jews of Rome.

Benjamin of Tudela visits Rome

A journey of six days from thence [Lucca] brings you to the large city of Rome, the metropolis of all Christendom. The two hundred Jews who live there are very much respected and pay tribute to no one. Some of them are officers in the service of Pope Alexander, who is the chief ecclesiastic and head of the Christian

church. The principal of the many eminent Jews resident here are R. Daniel and R. Jechiel. The latter is
one of the pope's officers, a handsome, prudent and
wise man, who frequents the pope's palace, being the
steward of his household and minister of his private
property. R. Jechiel is a descendant of R. Nathan, the
author of the Book Aruch and its comments. There
are further at Rome: R. Joab, son of Rabbi R. Sh'lomo;
R. Menachem, the president of the university; R.
Jechiel, who resides in Trastevere; and R. Benjamin,
son of R. Shabthai, of blessed memory.

The city of Rome is divided into two parts by means
of the river Tiber which runs through it. In the first
of these divisions you see the large place of worship
called St Peter of Rome, there was the large palace of
Julius Caesar. The city contains numerous buildings
and structures entirely different from all other buildings upon the face of the earth. The extent of ground
covered by the ruined and inhabited parts of Rome
amounts to four and twenty miles. You there find
eighty halls of the eighty eminent kings who are all
called Imperator, from King Tarquin to King Pepin,
the father of Charlemagne, who first conquered Spain
and wrested it from the Mahometans.

In the outskirts of Rome is the palace of Titus,
who was rejected by three hundred senators in consequence of his having wasted three years in the
conquest of Jerusalem, which task according to their

will he ought to have accomplished in two years.

Also St Giovanni in Porta Latina[3], in which place of worship there are two copper pillars constructed by King Solomon, of blessed memory, whose name, 'Solomon ben David' is engraved upon each. The Jews in Rome told him that every year about the time of the 9th of Ab[4], these pillars sweat so much that the water runs down from them.

You there see also the cave in which Titus the son of Vespasian hid the vessels of the temple, which he brought from Jerusalem[5]...

From *The Itinerary of Rabbi Benjamin of Tudela*, 12th century, Tr. A. Asher

John Evelyn witnesses a circumcision

I went to the Ghetto, where the Jews dwell, as in a suburb by themselves, being invited by a Jew of my acquaintance to see a circumcision. Here I passed by the Piazza Judea (where their seraglio begins) for being environ'd with walls, they are locked up every night...

Being led through the synagogue into a private house, I found a world of people in a chamber: by

---

3 Between the Baths of Caracalla and the beginning of the Via Appia.
4 The date of the destruction of the Temple.
5 Titus conquered Jerusalem in AD 70 and brought back the treasures from the Temple, which he placed in his so-called Temple of Peace, part of the Imperial Fora. A relief carving on the Arch of Titus in the Roman Forum shows the menorah, the seven-branched candlestick, being brought to Rome as booty.

and by came an old man who had prepared and laid in order divers instruments brought by a little child of about seven years old in a box. These the man laid in a silver basin: the knife was much like a short razor… Then they burnt some incense in a censer, which perfumed the room all the while the ceremony was doing. In the basin was also a little cap made of white paper like a Capuchins-hood, not bigger then my finger, also a paper of a red astringent powder, I suppose of bole: a small instrument of silver cleft in the midst, at one end to take up the prepuce withal, clouts of fine linen wrapped up &c. These all in order, the women from out of another chamber brought the infant swaddled, and delivered it to the Rabbi, who carried, and presented it before an altar…on which lay the five books of Moses, and the Commandments a little unrolled. Before this with profound reverence, and mumbling a few words he waved the child to and fro a while; then he delivered it to another Rabbi who sat all this time upon a table, he taking it in his hands put it between his thighs, whilst the other Jew unbound the blankets that were about it…at this action all the company fell a singing of an Hebrew hymn…The infant now stripped from the belly downwards, the Jew took the yard of the child and chafed it within his fingers till it became a little stiff, then with the silver instrument before described (which was held to him in the basin) he took up as much of the praeputium as he could possibly gather, and so with the razor, did rather saw than cut it off; at which the miserable babe cried extremely, while the rest continued their odd tone, rather like howling than singing. Then the Rabbi lifting the belly of the child to his face, and taking the yard all bloody into his mouth he sucked it a pretty while, having before taken a little vinegar, all which together with the blood he spit out into a glass of red wine of the colour of French wine. This done he stripped down the remainder of the foreskin as far and near to the belly as he could, so as it appeared to be all raw, then he strewed red powder on it to staunch the bleeding and covered it with a paper hood, and upon all a clout, and so swathed up the child as before. All this while they continue the Psalm. Then two of the women, and two men, viz, he who held the child, and the Rabbi who circumcised it (the rest I suppose were the witnesses) drank some of the wine mingled with the vinegar, blood and spittle...and the Rabbi cries out to me in the Italian tongue perceiving me to be a stranger: *Ecco Signior mio, un miracolo di dio*; because the child had immediately left crying.

From the *Diaries*, 15th January 1645

For Evelyn, travel writing is an impartial record of facts. He tells us that 'The Jews do all in Rome wear yellow hats, and live only upon brokerage and usury, very poor and despicable[6] beyond what they are in other territories of princes where they are permitted.' Two centuries later, we have arrived in the era of opinionated journalism. Hazlitt's reaction to the ghetto says as much about him as it does about Roman Jewry:

Hazlitt on the Ghetto

The Jews (I may add while I think of it) are shut up here in a quarter by themselves. I see no reason for it. It is a distinction not worth the making. There was a talk (it being Anno Santo[7]) of shutting them up for the whole of the present year. A soldier stands at the gate, to tell you that this is the Jews' quarter, and to take any thing you choose to give him for this piece of Christian information. A Catholic church[8] stands outside their prison, with a Crucifixion painted on it as a frontispiece, where they are obliged to hear a sermon in behalf of the truth of the Christian religion every Good Friday. On the same day they used to make them run races in the Corso, for the amusement of the rabble (high and low)—now they are compelled to provide horses for the same purpose. Owing to the politeness of the age, they no longer burn them as of yore, and that is something. Religious zeal, like all other things, grows old and feeble.

6 Despicable in the 17th-century sense, meaning poor, wretched.
7 A Holy Year, when pilgrims to Rome are granted special indulgences.
8 San Gregorio della Divina Pietà.

They treat the Jews in this manner at Rome (as a local courtesy to St Peter), and yet they compliment us on our increasing liberality to the Irish Catholics.

Notes of a Journey through France and Italy, 1826

The Bengali-American writer Jhumpa Lahiri sets one of her best short stories in Rome. It is the last of a trio of related narratives about two star-crossed lovers, Hema and Kaushik, who knew each other as children and meet again as adults, but too late to be able to alter the course of the destinies that beckon them both. Hema, a Classics professor, has borrowed a friend's apartment in the Ghetto in Rome. She is studying the Etruscans, but is also taking some time off, between the end of a dead-end love affair with a married academic and the beginning of an arranged marriage with Navin, a man she hardly knows in Calcutta:

Jhumpa Lahiri: a short story set in Rome

Saturday mornings, instead of working, she would go to the Campo de' Fiori, watching the stylish mothers in their high heels and jewels and quilted jackets pushing strollers and buying vegetables by the kilo. These women, with their rich, loose tangles of hair, their sunglasses concealing no wrinkles, were younger than Hema, but she felt inexperienced in their company, innocent of the responsibilities of rearing children and running a household and haggling flirtatiously with vegetable vendors. She had grown used to this feeling over the years with Julian—her position as the other woman, which had felt so sophisticated when their affair began, was actually a holding pen that kept her from growing up. She had denied herself the pleasure of openly sharing life with the person she loved, denied herself even the possibility of thinking about children. But Navin had changed that, too. They were both aware of her age, and as soon as they were married, Navin told her, he was eager to begin a family.

One day after lunch, feeling energetic, she walked all the way to Piazza del Popolo, and then over to the Villa Giulia for another visit[9]. In the museum she was moved once again by the ancient cups and spoons, still intact, that had once touched people's lips; the fibulae that had fastened their clothes, the thin wands with which they had applied perfume to their skin. But this time, looking at the giant sarcophagus of the bride and groom, enclosed in a box of glass, she found herself in tears. She couldn't help but think of Navin. Like the young smiling couple sitting affectionately on top of a shared casket, there was something dead about the marriage she was about to enter into. And though she knew it had every chance, over the years, of coming to life, on her way home, in the yellow

9 An old papal villa, now home to the Etruscan Museum.

light of evening, she was conscious only of its deadness. She shopped for her dinner in an *alimentari* on Via dei Giubbonari, and now she carried a bag containing lettuce, a box of spaghetti, and mushrooms and cream to turn into a sauce. She walked through the studded doorway of Giovanna's building, past a window like a ticket booth where one of two porters greeted her each day as she left and returned. In the courtyard a stone lion continually poured water from his mouth. And then up the stone steps, unlit, unyielding beneath her tired feet, three generous flights that felt like ten.

In the long hallway of Giovanna's apartment she saw the answering machine blinking. She played back the tape. It wasn't Navin's voice but a friend of Giovanna's. Normally these friends left messages in Italian that Giovanna retrieved from Berlin. But this message, in English, was for Hema. It was a person named Edo, a name she recognised from Giovanna's list of people to call. For weeks, Edo said in his message, he had been expecting Hema to get in touch. Was everything all right? He sounded kind, and genuinely distressed enough for Hema to return the call. She assured Edo that all was well, and because she had no other excuse she accepted his invitation to have lunch with him and his wife the following Sunday.

From 'Going Ashore' by Jhumpa Lahiri, in the short-story collection *Unaccustomed Earth*, 2008

THE SPANISH STEPS

In the 18th and 19th centuries every foreigner who came to Rome visited the Spanish Steps, and many of them had their lodging nearby. The area was a favoured haunt of *literati*, who patronised the Caffè Greco on Via Condotti. Goethe had rooms in the vicinity, as did the Brownings. Keats, of course, died there. Artists flocked to the area too: Rubens, Poussin, Sir Thomas Lawrence, Claude Lorrain, Edward Lear and John Flaxman all lived and worked here. The American sculptor William Wetmore Story, in his *Roba di Roma*, a collection of vignettes of Roman life, tells the popular story of Beppo the beggar, the 'Baron of the Spanish Steps'.

William Wetmore Story at the Spanish Steps

As one ascends to the last platform, before reaching the upper piazza in front of the Trinity de' Monti, a curious squat figure, with two withered and crumpled legs, spread out at right angles and clothed in long blue stockings, comes shuffling along on his knees and hands, which are protected by clogs. As it approaches, it turns suddenly up from its quadrupedal position, takes off its hat, shows a broad, stout, legless torso, with a vigorous chest and a ruddy face, as of a person who has come half-way up from below the steps through a trap-door, and with a smile whose breadth is equalled only by the cunning which lurks

round the corners of the eyes, says, in the blandest
and most patronising tones, with a rising inflection,
'*Buon giorno, Signore! Oggi fa bel tempo,*' or '*fa cattivo
tempo,*' as the case may be. This is no less a person
than Beppo, King of the Beggars, and Baron of the
Scale di Spagna. He is better known to travellers than
the Belvedere Torso of Hercules at the Vatican, and
has all the advantage over that wonderful work, of
having an admirable head and a good digestion. Hans
Christian Andersen has celebrated him in 'The Improvisatore', and unfairly attributed to him an infamous character and life; but this account is purely fic-
titious, and is neither *vero* nor *ben trovato*. Beppo, like
other distinguished personages, is not without a history. The Romans say of him, '*Era un Signore in paese
suo,*'—'He was a gentleman in his own country,'—and
this belief is borne out by a certain courtesy and style
in his bearing which would not shame the first gentlemen in the land. He was undoubtedly of a good
family in the provinces, and came to Rome, while yet
young, to seek his fortune. His crippled condition cut
him off from any active employment, and he adopted
the profession of a mendicant, as being the most lu-
crative and requiring the least exertion…After changing his name,—and, steadily pursuing this profession
for more than a quarter of a century, by dint of his
fair words, his bland smiles, and his constant '*Fa buon
tempo,*' and '*Fa cattivo tempo*' which, together with his

withered legs, were his sole stock in starting, he has finally amassed a very respectable little fortune. He is now about fifty-five years of age, has a wife and several children, and a few years ago, on the marriage of a daughter to a very respectable tradesman, he was able to give her what was considered in Rome a very respectable dowry.   From *Roba di Roma*, 1864

Edward Hutton on Piazza di Spagna

The Piazza di Spagna, that beautiful, irregular square, with its strange fountain before the Palace of the Spanish Embassy at the foot of the Spanish steps, remains, for the English certainly, the very centre of Rome, though indeed it is but just within the Aurelian wall. It is, in fact, one of the most characteristic places in the modern city, Papal so long, the key, as it were, to all the strangers' quarter, which still forms so important and even so indispensable a part of the old capital of the world. For without it Rome might seem indeed something less than eternal. Here at least we may see daily under our eyes her old power of drawing all men to her still in action, in spite of every transformation, in spite even of the fact that she, to whom the whole world was once but an antechamber, has now become the plaything of the youngest of the nations. Even yet in our crude thousands we come to her, to what end, for what help or message, in what need it would be difficult to explain. We come, and it is enough, and she who has ever dreamed of possessing the world first in her own behalf and then for the kingdom of Jesus, is content in her new rôle to see the actual rulers of the world astonished in her streets, dazzled by an outworn glory.

From *Rome*, 1924 (5th Ed.)

FESTIVALS & FEASTS

The most famous public spectacle in Rome in the 19th century was the Carnival celebration before Lent. Many writers have left descriptions of it, particularly of the processions along the Corso, when every balcony was filled with spectators and the street was jammed with people throwing flowers and sugar plums at each other. The culmination of the event was the *corsa* itself, the riderless horse race from Piazza del Popolo to Piazza Venezia. Not all visitors have enjoyed the Carnival. Henry James found it stupid. Charles Dickens loved it.

Charles Dickens on the Carnival

The Friday and Saturday having been solemn Festa days, and Sunday being always a DIES NON in carnival proceedings, we had looked forward, with some impatience and curiosity, to the beginning of the new week: Monday and Tuesday being the two last and best days of the Carnival.

On the Monday afternoon at one or two o'clock, there began to be a great rattling of carriages into the court-yard of the hotel; a hurrying to and fro of all the servants in it; and, now and then, a swift shooting across some doorway or balcony, of a straggling stranger in a fancy dress: not yet sufficiently well used to the same to wear it with confidence and defy public opinion. All the carriages were open, and had the linings carefully covered with white cotton or calico, to prevent their proper decorations from being spoiled by the incessant pelting of sugar-plums; and people were packing and cramming into every vehicle as it waited for its occupants, enormous sacks and baskets full of these confetti, together with such heaps of flowers, tied up in little nosegays, that some carriages were not only brimful of flowers, but literally running over: scattering, at every shake and jerk of the springs, some of their abundance on the ground. Not to be behindhand in these essential particulars, we caused two very respectable sacks of sugar-plums (each about three feet high) and a large clothesbasket full of flowers to be conveyed into our hired barouche, with all speed. And from our place of observation, in one of the upper balconies of the hotel, we contemplated these arrangements with the liveliest satisfaction. The carriages now beginning to take up their company, and move away, we got into ours, and drove off too, armed with little wire masks for our faces; the sugar-plums, like Falstaff's adulterated sack, having lime in their composition…

We fell into the string of coaches, and, for some time, jogged on quietly enough; now crawling on at a very slow walk; now trotting half-a-dozen yards; now backing fifty; and now stopping altogether: as the pressure in front obliged us…Occasionally, we interchanged a volley of confetti with the carriage next in front, or the carriage next behind…Presently, we came into a narrow street, where, besides one line of carriages going, there was another line of carriages returning. Here the sugar-plums and the nosegays began to fly about, pretty smartly…Some quarter of an hour of this sort of progress, brought us to the Corso; and anything so gay, so bright, and lively as the whole scene there, it would be difficult to imagine. From all the innumerable balconies: from the remotest and highest, no less than from the lowest and nearest: hangings of bright red, bright green, bright blue, white and gold, were fluttering in the brilliant sunlight. From windows, and from parapets, and tops of houses, streamers of the richest colours, and draperies of the gaudiest and most sparkling hues, were floating out upon the street. The buildings seemed to have been literally turned inside out, and to have all their gaiety towards the highway. Shop-fronts were taken down, and the windows filled with company, like boxes at a shining theatre…and in every nook

and corner, from the pavement to the chimney-tops,
where women's eyes could glisten, there they danced,
and laughed, and sparkled, like the light in water.

From *Pictures from Italy*, 1846

After a serious accident in 1882, *The New York Times*
adopted a disapproving attitude towards the Carnival,
as the following reports show:

The New York Times disapproves of the Carnival

A sad accident attended the close of the recent carnival festivities in Rome. When the Corso was supposed to have been cleared at 5:30 the *barberi*, or
riderless horses, goaded by spiked balls swinging on
their haunches, were let loose at the Piazza del Popolo and started toward the goal in the Piazza Venezia at a furious speed. When they reached Palazzo
Fiano, just below the Queen's balcony, the crowd
still thronged the street and the horses plunged into
it, knocking down men, women, and children. The
Queen fell back sickened at the sight and one of her
ladies of honor fainted. Thirteen persons were found
to have been seriously injured, one of whom died
immediately, his head having been crushed, and
another the next morning. The King witnessed the
scene from a neighbouring balcony and visited the
sufferers after they had been taken to the hospitals,
spending an hour with them. Roman newspapers

denounce this form of sport as brutal and call for its abolition. *New York Times*, 9th March 1882

Six days later, the same newspaper was holding forth in the following vein:

The Italian carnival, which, for the last twenty-four years, has been the dullest of all possible amusements, is now rapidly becoming a nuisance. There undoubtedly was a time when the carnival had an excuse for being. It gave a sense of license, if not of liberty, to the subjects of the old despotic Governments, and it afforded admirable opportunities for the pursuit of the intrigues and adventures which— if we may believe contemporary writers like the veracious M. CASANOVA—constituted the sole occupation of Italian gentlemen. But in the nineteenth century the carnival is as utter an anachronism as is the procession in honor of DIONYSUS, which still survives among the descendants of the Greek colonists in certain Calabrian towns. Of late years the carnival in Rome...was chiefly the work of foreign visitors. Englishmen, Americans, Germans, and Russians hired balconies on the Corso, or drove up and down that venerable avenue in carriages, and fancied that when they threw bits of colored lime or bundles of withered flowers at one another they were taking part in a characteristic Italian festival...

A few years ago an enterprising person attempted to introduce the carnival in [New York]. His conception of a carnival was a procession of tradesmen's wagons covered with advertisements, and a masked ball for which the public should buy tickets…Dreary as the New York carnival was, it was not so entirely idiotic as the Italian carnival, and the Italians might substitute something of the sort for the amusement and instruction of their foreign visitors. A Roman procession, made up of Roman shop-keepers displaying their wares, would be at least as interesting as a procession of Englishmen in wire masks and Americans dressed in stripes and star-spangled garments. Advertisements, neatly rolled together, could be thrown at people with much less disagreeable consequences than those which sometimes attend the throwing of lime pellets…

Of course, such a carnival would have nothing of romance about it, but the Italians are rapidly discovering that their age of romance is over, and that life in the latter part of the nineteenth century and under a free government must be prosaic if it is to be profitable. Either they must banish the carnival altogether or they must make it a purely business affair, hard as either alternative will be to the young Americans who want to dress themselves in the Stars and Stripes and enjoy themselves 'after the Italian manner'.

The New York Times, 15th March 1882

While the Romans of the ancient Republic were known for their frugality and prided themselves on not being nice in diet (Cato the Censor was shocked when he learned that a good horse cost less than a cook), the Imperial era was known for its feasting, and Latin authors make frequent mention of banquets. The 1st-century BC scholar Marcus Terentius Varro left a description of the ideal dinner party. Not all the dishes served at such feasts were as elaborate as the emperor Vitellius' legendary 'Shield of Minerva', which combined pike's liver, flamingoes' tongues, peacocks' brains and the sperm glands of lampreys. Nevertheless, not many years before Vitellius' reign (he ruled for eight months in AD 69) Seneca was lamenting that the city had grown luxurious:

Seneca on too much holiday-making

It is the month of December and the city is in a great sweat. License has been granted to public luxury. Elaborate and noisy preparations are underway, as if the Saturnalia were just a working day like any other. Truly, it has become so, to the extent that I can only agree with whoever said that December was once just a month but is now a whole year. If I had you with me I would love to discuss what should be done: should we make no change at all to our daily round; or, so as not to seem out of step with public custom, should we strip off our togas and throw riotous dinners? Whereas once it was normal only to change our garb in times of unrest or hardship, it's now happening purely for pleasure and feast days.

Moral Epistles Book I, 18, 1st century AD (Tr. AB)

The perfect Roman dinner party

Marcus Varro, in a treatise of the disposition and order of an elegant banquet, the choice, condition, and qualities of the guests, begins first with their number, which, he says, should not be less than the graces, nor more than the muses. They ought not to be many, that every person may have his turn to speak, as well as to hear. A large company is subject to noise and confusion; and a number of equals cannot be restrained within the bounds of decency and respect toward each other.

Four things, he says, are requisite toward an elegant entertainment.—The guests must be of some quality, well-bred, and well-dressed: the place retired from public view, and all disturbances of passengers or business, where the company may hear nothing, but what proceeds from themselves: the time convenient, neither too late nor too early; for an early supper follows too soon upon dinner, and a late one breaks in upon our hours of rest, as well as the business of the next day: the apartment, attendants, and whole apparatus for the feast, rather neat, than fine; elegant, than rich; and the entertainment such as the invited may afford each in their turns.

The company should not be great talkers, nor too silent; but ingenious persons, knowing when to speak, and when to listen; rather facetious and witty than argumentative or rhetorical. Eloquence is proper for a senate, and disputation may be necessary at the bar; but a more concise expression, and quicker repartee, are fitter talents for familiar converse.

The guests should neither be all old, nor all young men; for the one talk of nothing but former times… and the other only speak of present debauches or amours. Upon such meetings, the old should assume an air of youth, and the young ought to comport themselves with a *pro tempore* gravity; which will bring the extremes to meet, in an happy and social medium…

Stories should be rarely introduced, because they prevent the freedom of conversation too long…The discourse ought never turn upon politics, private concerns, or subjects in which any of the company are at all interested…nothing should be spoken of, but such pleasing and improving topics as beauty, painting, music, poetry, or the ancient and modern writers: by which charming themes we may both exercise and exalt our genius, instead of puzzling and straining the mind with abstruse positions, or contentious arguments, which arise frequently from an affectation of superior knowledge, and is the worst effect, as well as the surest sign, of self-sufficiency. Such persons often conclude themselves in the right, because others choose to spare themselves the idle trouble of proving them in the wrong...

To conclude, every guest ought to be left at liberty, both in wine as well as meat; for it is among men, as among horses, the bridle is required to some, and the spur to others.

From *The London Magazine, or Gentlemen's Monthly Intelligencer*, 1767

One of the most famous Roman dinners ever described is the feast of Trimalchio, the vulgar freedman, in Petronius' *Satyricon*. The work is a prose satire from the time of Nero, to whom Petronius was *arbiter elegantiarum*, judge of taste. Nero was addicted to writing verses, which he would perform in public, at desperate length, to an audience forbidden to leave. There are stories of women feigning the pangs of childbirth in order to escape from the auditorium. In his *Quo Vadis* (*see p. 49*), Henryk Sienkiewicz includes a sene where Petronius presents a copy of the *Satyricon* to his nephew:

'Here is a gift for thee,' said [Petronius].

'Thanks!' answered Vinicius. Then, looking at the title, he inquired, "Satyricon"? Is this something new? Whose is it?'

'Mine. But...no one knows of this, and do thou mention it to no man.'

'Thou hast said that thou art no writer of verses,' said

Vinicius, looking at the middle of the manuscript; 'but here I see prose thickly interwoven with them.'

'When thou art reading, turn attention to Trimalchion's feast. As to verses, they have disgusted me, since Nero is writing an epic. Vitellius[10], when he wishes to relieve himself, uses ivory fingers to thrust down his throat; others serve themselves with flamingo feathers steeped in olive oil or in a decoction of wild thyme. I read Nero's poetry, and the result is immediate. Straightway I am able to praise it, if not with a clear conscience, at least with a clear stomach.'

Though not in fact set in Rome (the story takes place in Campania, on the Bay of Naples), an extract from Petronius' original is quoted here for the picture it gives of the elaborate banquets that were held in the houses of the rich and nouveau-riche:

Trimalchio's feast

Thus was the table resounding to our wit when Trimalchio came back in, dabbing his brow and washing his hands in balm. After a short pause, he said, 'Forgive me, my friends, but my stomach's been playing up for days. Not even the doctors knew what to do. But I've had great relief from pomegran-

10 The same *grand gourmand* who invented the Shield of Minerva (*see p. 71*) and who later became emperor.

ate rind and pine resin in vinegar. I hope my insides will behave themselves now. Sometimes there's such a rumbling in my guts you'd think there was a bull in there. So if any of you feel like doing your business, please don't be shy. None of us is born solid and I don't know of any worse torture than holding it in—not even Jupiter can contain it. Are you laughing, Fortunata? As if you haven't kept me awake many a night! Well, no guest in any dining-room of mine is forbidden from responding to the call of nature and the doctors say we should let it go free. So if you're caught short, everything's ready outside: water, commodes, and other requisites. Believe me, if you let your wind rise to your brain your whole body will be in a flux. I know plenty that have died because they were too shy to speak out.'

We thanked him for his thoughtful generosity, hiding our laughter in our wine cups. Little did we realise that we were only halfway through dinner, still on the uphill section, as they say. For when the tables had been cleared, to a fanfare of music, three white pigs were led into the dining-room, muzzled and hung with little bells. One of these, so the *nomenclator* announced, was two years old, another three and the third six. I thought they were performing porkers, like the kind one sees at the circus, and that they were about to do some tricks. But Trimalchio disabused us by asking, 'Which of these do you want for dinner now? Anyone can do countryfied chicken and that kind of slop, but my cooks are used to preparing calves boiled whole.' He then had the chef brought in, and without waiting to hear our choice ordered that the eldest be killed and asked peremptorily,

'Which division are you from?'

When the chef replied that he was from the fortieth, Trimalchio went on, 'Did I buy you or were you born into my household?'

'Neither. I was left to you in Pansa's will.'

'Well see you do a good job or I'll have you relegated to the rank of messenger-boy.'

Thus suitably admonished, the chef led our next course back to the kitchen.

Trimalchio then became genial as he turned to us. 'I'll change the wine if you don't like it,' he said, 'but otherwise please do me the favour of drinking it. I don't buy it, thanked be the gods. I now produce all my palate-ticklers on my suburban estate. I've not seen it yet, but they tell me it's down Terracina and Tarentum way. I'm toying with the idea of adding Sicily to my holdings, so if ever I go to Africa I can just sail along my own garden fence, as it were…'

From the *Satyricon*, by Petronius Arbiter, mid-1st century AD (Tr. AB)

THE COLOSSEUM

'While the Colosseum stands, Rome shall stand; when the Colosseum falls, Rome shall fall; and when Rome falls, the world.'
Ancient proverb

The Colosseum *is* falling down. Three slabs of ancient plaster fell from one of the entrance arches in the summer of 2010. What is to be done? This is the most iconic ruin in Rome, the largest amphitheatre ever built in the ancient Empire, scene of the deaths, at is inaugural games, of nine thousand beasts and who knows how many gladiators. Its true name is the Flavian Amphitheatre, because it was built during the reigns of two emperors of the Flavian dynasty, Vespasian and Titus, between AD 70 and 80. The name Colosseum comes from a colossal statue of Nero, in the guise of the sun-god Apollo, which stood beside it, in a place which had formerly been the atrium to his sumptuous Domus Aurea, the Golden House, which stretched for half a square kilometre in the very heart of the city, and whose gilded and painted halls, Nero is supposed to have claimed, made him 'finally feel he was being housed like a human being'. When this most depraved of all the emperors, murderer of his own mother as well as of his second wife,

finally took his own life, his successors tore down the
Golden House and restored the land to the city, building
public baths and an enormous arena on the site. This
fact is celebrated by the satirist Martial, in a poem that
formed part of his *Liber Spectaculorum*, published to co-
incide with the inauguration of the Colosseum:

Martial praises the Colosseum

Here where the stellar Colossus scans the very stars
    And the cranes loom tall in the roadway
Once gleamed the odious halls of a rabid king—
    The only house that stood in the whole of Rome.
On the spot where the Amphitheatre's august mound
    Heaves into view, just there, was Nero's lake;
And there, where we gaze on the gift of thermal baths
    A park had turned men out of house and home.
The limit of those never-ended halls stood where
    The Claudian porch now casts its spreading shade.
Rome is restored to herself, and Caesar[1], under you
    What once were a lord's, are now the people's
                                        pleasures.
            Liber Spectaculorum II, 1st century AD (Tr. AB)

Though Seneca never attended games in the Colosseum
(in his day, it had not been built), he saw gladiator fights
and wild animal hunts in other arenas, and in one of

---

1 The emperor Titus, under whom the Colosseum was inaugurated.

his letters urged a friend to stay away from the games, because 'you must be either corrupted by the mob, or, if you show your revulsion, reviled by them'. He surely had a point. Amphitheatres hosted the most pitiless sights, particularly in the later Empire, when emperors were increasingly reliant on mob support to keep them in power. They courted popularity by staging ever more elaborately bizarre and revolting spectacles. Here is Martial again, with a satirical verse to prove the point:

> Pasiphaë DID sleep with the Cretan bull[2]. Trust me,
>   We've seen it. The old myth's been proved true.
> Antiquity, O Caesar, needn't be so revered:
>   Whatever fame sings of, the arena offers you.
>   *Liber Spectaculorum* V, 1st century AD (Tr. AB)

Sponsors of the games became ever keener to find new extravagances to show people, and more exotic animals to drive to their deaths to amuse them. Whole provinces were denuded of their wildlife—the North African elephant (the type that Hannibal had used) was driven to extinction, purely to feed the arena. Men and animals were butchered in appalling numbers. And for bored Roman housewives, gladiators became sex symbols. Even women began entering the arena, as

---

2 Pasiphaë was the wife of Minos, King of Crete. She conceived a passion for a bull and the result of this bestial union, according to legend, was the Minotaur.

the historian Cassius Dio tells us, in this piece about the reign of Titus:

Cassius Dio on the spectacles in the arena

In dedicating the hunting-theatre and the baths that bear his name, [Titus] produced many remarkable spectacles. There was a battle between cranes and also between four elephants; animals both tame and wild were slain to the number of nine thousand; and women (not those of any prominence, however) took part in despatching them. As for the men, several fought in single combat and several groups contended together both in infantry and naval battles. For Titus suddenly filled this same theatre with water and brought in horses and bulls and some other domesticated animals that had been taught to behave in the liquid element just as on land. He also brought in people on ships, who engaged in a sea-fight there… and others gave a similar exhibition outside the city in the grove of Gaius and Lucius, a place which Augustus had once excavated for this very purpose. There, too, on the first day there was a gladiatorial exhibition and wild-beast hunt, the lake in front of the images having first been covered over with a platform of planks and wooden stands erected around it. On the second day there was a horse-race, and on the third day a naval battle between three thousand men, followed by an infantry battle. The 'Athenians' conquered the 'Syracusans' (these were the names the combatants used), made a landing on the islet and assaulted and captured a wall that had been constructed around the monument. These were the spectacles that were offered, and they continued for a hundred days; but Titus also furnished some things that were of practical use to the people. He would throw down into the theatre from aloft little wooden balls variously inscribed, one designating some article of food, another clothing, another a silver vessel or perhaps a gold one, or again horses, pack-animals, cattle or slaves. Those who seized them were to carry them to the dispensers of the bounty, from whom they would receive the article named.

Roman History LXVI, 3rd century AD, Tr. E. Cary

MODERN WRITERS ON THE COLOSSEUM

For modern writers the Colosseum is one of the great set pieces of Rome. All have attempted to evoke its atmosphere, in letters, diaries and poetry. In the early part of the 19th century the Colosseum was still unexcavated, and many writers left enthusiastic descriptions of the flowers and plants, some of them rare, that found a congenial habitat among its stones. Fewer authors than one might expect seem to have been impressed by the building's blood-soaked history. They all visited it, to be sure, and stood within its walls and shuddered. But many authors of the Romantic age were too preoccupied by reflections on the noble race of the ancients and scorn for the Dark Ages which had succeeded them. Shelley was enormously inspired by the Colosseum. He visited it, as he wrote to Peacock in 1818, 'day after day' and found it 'unlike any work of human hands I ever saw before...It has been changed by time into the image of an amphitheatre of rocky hills overgrown by the wild olive, the myrtle and the fig-tree, and threaded by little paths, which wind among its ruined stairs and immeasurable galleries...The interior is all ruin. I can scarcely believe that when encrusted with Dorian marble and ornamented by columns of Egyptian granite, its effect could have been so sublime and so impressive as in its present state'. The spirit of the place, he believed, far from appalling us with remembered brutality, has softened the edges of past savagery and left us with something more permanent and important, a sense of the 'broad and everlasting character of human strength and genius'. This was Shelley being deliberately anti-Byronic. He was determined only to see the grandeur of the ruin, whereas Byron had also seen its horror. One of the most famous lines ever written about the Colosseum is Byron's, when he describes a gladiator as 'butcher'd to make a Roman holiday' (*see p. 86*).

Smollett is typically robust in his attitude (*see overleaf*). Stendhal, though he deplored the butchery that had taken place there, was so impatient to get to the Colosseum that he paid too much for his rooms on Via Gregoriana ('at a moment like this, how can one occupy oneself with such tiny concerns?…It is the most beautiful of ruins, it breathes all the majesty of ancient Rome.').

The spectacle of the ruins by moonlight was especially popular, in the days when it was still possible to wander in after dark. The poet Stephen Spender went there twice at midnight, claiming that he had 'come to like the Coliseum at this hour better than any other'. J.B.S. Morritt, writing in the 1790s, felt the same:

J.B.S. Morritt on the Colosseum by moonlight

A still more favourite sight of mine has been the Coliseum by moonlight. You have seen descriptions over and over of this enormous ruin of the Flavian Amphitheatre. Half of it is nearly entire, and the rest, broken into beauty by time, and overgrown with bushes, was lighted up or through into masses of deep shade by one of the finest moonlight nights ever beheld.

Letter to his aunt, 29th March 1796

Smollett on the Colosseum

The Colossaeum or amphitheatre…is the most stupendous work of the kind which antiquity can produce. Near one half of the external circuit still remains, consisting of four tiers of arcades, adorned with columns of four orders, Doric, Ionic, Corinthian, and Composite...The Colossaeum was built by Vespasian, who employed thirty thousand Jewish slaves in the work; but finished and dedicated by his son Titus, who, on the first day of its being opened, produced fifty thousand wild beasts, which were all killed in the arena.

The Romans were undoubtedly a barbarous people, who delighted in horrible spectacles...They took delight in seeing their fellow-creatures torn in pieces by wild beasts, in the amphitheatre. They shouted with applause when they saw a poor dwarf or slave killed by his adversary; but their transports were altogether extravagant when the devoted captives were obliged to fight in troops, till one side was entirely butchered by the other. Nero produced four hundred senators, and six hundred of the equestrian order, as gladiators in the public arena: even the women fought with wild beasts, as well as with each other, and drenched the amphitheatres with their blood...It is not at all clear to me, that a people is the more brave, the more they are accustomed to bloodshed in their public entertainments. True bravery is not savage but humane.

From *Travels through France and Italy*, 1766

Byron on the Colosseum

And here the buzz of eager nations ran,
In murmur'd pity, or loud-roar'd applause,
As man was slaughter'd by his fellow man.

And wherefore slaughter'd? wherefore, but because
Such were the bloody Circus' genial laws,
And the imperial pleasure.—Wherefore not?
What matters where we fall to fill the maws
Of worms—on battle-plains or listed spot?
Both are but theatres where the chief actors rot.

I see before me the Gladiator lie:
He leans upon his hand—his manly brow
Consents to death, but conquers agony,
And his droop'd head sinks gradually low—
And through his side the last drops, ebbing slow
From the red gash, fall heavy, one by one,
Like the first of a thunder-shower; and now
The arena swims around him—he is gone,
Ere ceased the inhuman shout which hail'd the
                                      wretch who won.

He heard it, but he heeded not—his eyes
Were with his heart, and that was far away:
He reck'd not of the life he lost nor prize,
But where his rude hut by the Danube lay,
There were his young barbarians all at play,
There was their Dacian mother—he, their sire,
Butcher'd to make a Roman holiday—
All this rush'd with his blood—Shall he expire
And unavenged?—Arise! ye Goths, and glut your ire!

But here, where Murder breathed her bloody steam;
And here, where buzzing nations choked the ways,
And roar'd or murmur'd like a mountain stream
Dashing or winding as its torrent strays;
Here, where the Roman millions' blame or praise
Was death or life, the playthings of a crowd,
My voice sounds much, and fall the stars' faint rays
On the arena void—seats crush'd—walls bow'd—
And galleries, where my steps seem echoes
strangely loud.
From *Childe Harold's Pilgrimage* Canto IV, 1818

Stendhal on the Colosseum

The Colosseum is built almost entirely of blocks of travertine, a decidedly ugly stone, filled with holes like tufa and of a whiteness tending to yellow. It was brought from Tivoli. The aspect of all the monuments of Rome would be more pleasing to the initial glance if the architects had had at their disposal the lovely stone that is used at Lyon or Edinburgh, or even the marble of which the circus of Pula (Dalmatia) is made.

Below the Doric arches of the Colosseum are ancient numbers; each one of these archways served as an entrance. Numerous stairways led to the upper tiers and porticoes. Thus in only a few instants a hundred thousand spectators could enter and leave the Colosseum. It is said that Titus had a tunnel built from his palace on the Esquiline Hill, which allowed him to enter the Colosseum without appearing in the streets of Rome. This tunnel is said to have come in between arches 38 and 39. There, indeed, one sees an unnumbered archway...

From *Promenades dans Rome*, 1829 (Tr. AB)

THE COLOSSEUM IN FICTION

Numerous novels include a scene within the Colosseum's walls. Two of its most memorable appearances occur in the work of American writers, the friends Edith Wharton and Henry James. In Wharton's short story *Roman Fever*, two elderly ladies reminisce about their youth in Rome. It transpires over the course of their conversation that they had been rivals in love: as the story unfolds we learn of a revenge plot gone wrong as one of the ladies is forced to realise that, far from having triumphed over her rival by marrying the man they both loved, she was in fact the loser in the game:

Edith Wharton on an assignation at the Colosseum

'The story of your wicked aunt made such an impression on me. And I thought: "There's no more Roman fever, but the Forum is deathly cold after sunset—especially after a hot day. And the Colosseum's even colder and damper." '

'The Colosseum—?'

'Yes. It wasn't easy to get in, after the gates were locked for the night. Far from easy. Still, in those days it could be managed; it was managed, often. Lovers met there who couldn't meet elsewhere. You knew that?'

'I—I daresay. I don't remember.'

'You don't remember? You don't remember going to visit some ruins or other one evening, just after dark, and catching a bad chill! You were supposed to have gone to see the moonrise. People always said that expedition was what caused your illness.'

There was a moment's silence; then Mrs Ansley rejoined: 'Did they? It was all so long ago.'

'Yes. And you got well again—so it didn't matter. But I suppose it struck your friends—the reason given for your illness. I mean—because everybody knew you were so prudent on account of your throat, and your mother took such care of you... You had been out late sightseeing, hadn't you, that night.'

'Perhaps I had. The most prudent girls aren't always prudent. What made you think of it now?'

Mrs Slade seemed to have no answer ready. But after a moment she broke out: 'Because I simply can't bear it any longer—'

Mrs Ansley lifted her head quickly. Her eyes were wide and very pale. 'Can't bear what?'

'Why—your not knowing that I've always known why you went.'

'Why I went—?'

'Yes. You think I'm bluffing, don't you? Well, you went to meet the man I was engaged to—and I can repeat every word of the letter that took you there.'

While Mrs Slade spoke Mrs Ansley had risen unsteadily to her feet. Her bag, her knitting and gloves, slid in a panic-stricken heap to the ground. She looked at Mrs Slade as though she were looking at a ghost.

'No, no—don't,' she faltered out.

'Why not? Listen, if you don't believe me. "My one darling, things can't go on like this. I must see you alone. Come to the Colosseum immediately after dark tomorrow. There will be somebody to let you in. No one whom you need fear will suspect"—but perhaps you've forgotten what the letter said?'

Mrs Ansley met the challenge with an unexpected composure. Steadying herself against the chair she looked at her friend, and replied: 'No; I know it by heart too.'

'And the signature? "Only your D.S." Was that it? I'm right, am I? That was the letter that took you out that evening after dark?'

Mrs Ansley was still looking at her. It seemed to Mrs Slade that a slow struggle was going on behind the voluntarily controlled mask of her small quiet face. 'I shouldn't have thought she had herself so well in hand,' Mrs Slade reflected, almost resentfully. But at this moment Mrs Ansley spoke. 'I don't know how you knew. I burned that letter at once.'

'Yes; you would, naturally—you're so prudent!' The sneer was open now. 'And if you burned the letter you're wondering how on earth I know what was in it. That's it, isn't it?'

Mrs Slade waited, but Mrs Ansley did not speak.

'Well, my dear, I know what was in that letter because I wrote it!'

'You wrote it?'

'Yes.'

The two women stood for a minute staring at each other in the last golden light. Then Mrs Ansley dropped back into her chair. 'Oh,' she murmured, and covered her face with her hands...

From Roman Fever, 1934

The Colosseum plays an important role in Henry James' *Daisy Miller*, the story of a pretty young American girl on a European tour with her mother and younger brother. In Switzerland she meets Mr Winterbourne, through whose eyes the narrative unfolds. He is captivated by Daisy, but puzzled. Her manners are very frank and very free. She is unlike other women. She pays no heed to the rules of chaperone. She makes no distinction between female friends and male, and has no compunction about going off for a day's sightseeing alone with a man. Society frowns on such antics, but it never enters Daisy's head that there can be anything wrong in it. Her mother is weak and silly and cannot guide her. Daisy is completely unwilling to guide herself; her spirit is too independent. In the end, her behaviour catches up with her. The matrons of the expatriate salons in Rome do not like it. On one famous occasion the hostess refuses to acknowledge her. Winterbourne at last resolves to speak to her mother, to warn her that her daughter is damaging that thing called reputation, so important to a young lady if she is not to be ostracised by society—which is, after all, the only milieu that a human being can inhabit. But Mrs Miller is powerless to influence her daughter. Daisy continues to be seen around town with her Italian friend, Mr Giovanelli. One night Winterbourne encounters them in the Colosseum:

Daisy Miller at the Colosseum

A week afterward [Winterbourne] went to dine at a beautiful villa on the Caelian Hill, and, on arriving, dismissed his hired vehicle. The evening was charming, and he promised himself the satisfaction of walking home beneath the Arch of Constantine and past the vaguely lighted monuments of the Forum. There was a waning moon in the sky, and her radiance was not brilliant, but she was veiled in a thin cloud curtain which seemed to diffuse and equalise it. When, on his return from the villa (it was eleven o'clock), Winterbourne approached the dusky circle of the Colosseum, it occurred to him, as a lover of the picturesque, that the interior, in the pale moonshine, would be well worth a glance. He turned aside and walked to one of the empty arches, near which, as he observed, an open carriage—one of the little Roman streetcabs—was stationed. Then he passed in, among the cavernous shadows of the great structure, and emerged upon the clear and silent arena. The place had never seemed to him more impressive. One half of the gigantic circus was in deep shade, the other was sleeping in the luminous dusk. As he stood there he began to murmur Byron's famous lines, out of 'Manfred'[3], but before he had finished his quotation he remembered that if nocturnal meditations in the Colosseum are recommended by the poets, they are deprecated by the doctors. The historic atmosphere was there, certainly; but the historic atmosphere, scientifically considered, was no better than a villainous miasma. Winterbourne walked to the middle of the arena, to take a more general glance, intending thereafter to make a hasty retreat. The great cross in the centre was covered with shadow; it was only as he drew near it that he made it out distinctly. Then he saw that two persons were stationed upon the low steps which formed its base. One of these was a woman, seated; her companion was standing in front of her.

3 'Upon such a night / I stood within the Coliseum's wall / Midst the chief relics of almighty Rome...'

Presently the sound of the woman's voice came to him distinctly in the warm night air. 'Well, he looks at us as one of the old lions or tigers may have looked at the Christian martyrs!' These were the words he heard, in the familiar accent of Miss Daisy Miller.

'Let us hope he is not very hungry,' responded the ingenious Giovanelli. 'He will have to take me first; you will serve for dessert!'

Winterbourne stopped, with a sort of horror, and, it must be added, with a sort of relief. It was as if a sudden illumination had been flashed upon the ambiguity of Daisy's behaviour, and the riddle had become easy to read. She was a young lady whom a gentleman need no longer be at pains to respect. He stood there, looking at her—looking at her companion and not reflecting that though he saw them vaguely, he himself must have been more brightly visible. He felt angry with himself that he had bothered so much about the right way of regarding Miss Daisy Miller. Then, as he was going to advance again, he checked himself, not from the fear that he was doing her injustice, but from a sense of the danger of appearing unbecomingly exhilarated by this sudden revulsion from cautious criticism. He turned away toward the entrance of the place, but, as he did so, he heard Daisy speak again.

'Why, it was Mr Winterbourne! He saw me, and he cuts me!'

What a clever little reprobate she was, and how

smartly she played at injured innocence! But he wouldn't cut her. Winterbourne came forward again and went toward the great cross. Daisy had got up; Giovanelli lifted his hat. Winterbourne had now begun to think simply of the craziness, from a sanitary point of view, of a delicate young girl lounging away the evening in this nest of malaria. What if she were a clever little reprobate? that was no reason for her dying of the *perniciosa*. 'How long have you been here?' he asked almost brutally.

Daisy, lovely in the flattering moonlight, looked at him a moment. Then—'All the evening,' she answered, gently… 'I never saw anything so pretty.'

'I am afraid,' said Winterbourne, 'that you will not think Roman fever very pretty. This is the way people catch it. I wonder,' he added, turning to Giovanelli, 'that you, a native Roman, should countenance such a terrible indiscretion.'

'Ah,' said the handsome native, 'for myself I am not afraid.'

'Neither am I—for you! I am speaking for this young lady.'

Giovanelli lifted his well-shaped eyebrows and showed his brilliant teeth. But he took Winterbourne's rebuke with docility. 'I told the signorina it was a grave indiscretion, but when was the signorina ever prudent?'

From *Daisy Miller*, 1878

ROME & RELIGION

'What man exists who does not know that this city was founded by the auspices; that the auspices were consulted before anything was done, either at home or on the battlefield?'
Livy, *Ab Urbe Condita* Book VI,
1st century BC, (Tr. AB)'

Rome can claim to have given the world law and order, a political system and a pattern for its civic buildings. It has also presided over another unifying force: religion. The Roman form of worship, with its pantheon of gods, its festivals and its deified emperors, was imposed across the Empire, but it was done carefully, adopting and adapting elements from the religions of the conquered peoples. Devotional customs and divinities from many civilisations—the Etruscans, the Phoenicians, the Egyptians, the Persians—were assimilated and given a Roman guise, and many of these imported cults were extremely popular. Judaism came to Rome too: the Jewish community there is the oldest in the world outside the Holy Land.

The customs of analysing entrails and watching the flight of birds for omens came to Rome from the Etruscans. Thornton Wilder, in his historical novel-in-letters

The Ides of March, portrays the sceptical Julius Caesar, poised to rule the Empire as dictator, and yet reluctant to be seen as disrespectful of superstitious observance:

Thornton Wilder on the hocus-pocus of soothsayers

I enclose in this week's packet a half-dozen of the innumerable reports which, as Supreme Pontiff, I receive from the Augurs, Soothsayers, Sky Watchers, and Chicken Nurses.

I enclose also the directions I have issued for the monthly Commemoration of the Founding of the City.

What's to be done?

I have inherited this burden of superstition and nonsense. I govern innumerable men but must acknowledge that I am governed by birds and thunderclaps.

All this frequently obstructs the operation of the State; it closes the doors of the Senate and the Courts for days and weeks at a time. It employs several thousands of persons. Everyone who has anything to do with it, including the Supreme Pontiff, manipulates it to his own interest.

One afternoon, in the Rhine Valley, the augurs of our headquarters forbade me to join battle with the enemy. It seems that our sacred chickens were eating fastidiously. Mesdames Partlet were crossing their feet as they walked; they were frequently inspecting the sky and looking back over their shoulders, and with good reason. I too on entering the valley had been

discouraged to observe that it was the haunt of eagles. We generals are reduced to viewing the sky with
a chicken's eyes. I acceded for one day, though in my
capability of surprising the enemy lay one of my few
advantages, and I feared that I would be similarly im-
peded in the morning. That evening, however, Asinius Pollio and I took a walk in the woods; we gathered
a dozen grubs; we minced them into fine pieces with
our knives and strewed them about the sacred feed-
ing-pen. The next morning the entire army waited in
suspense to hear the will of the Gods. The fateful birds
were put out to feed. They first surveyed the sky emitting that chirp of alarm which is sufficient to arrest ten
thousand men; then they turned their gaze upon their
meal. By Hercules, their eyes protruded; they uttered
cries of ravished gluttony; they flew to their repast,
and I was permitted to win the battle of Cologne.

From *The Ides of March*, 1948

THE CULT OF CHRISTIANITY

One of the most persistent of the foreign cults imported to ancient Rome was that of a Jew named Jesus
Christ. The emperor Constantine made persecution of
his followers illegal in 313. Later he converted to the
Christian faith himself. With imperial sanction the new
religion, in its outward forms at least, adopted much

from the state religion of pagan Rome—its basilicas (as churches), its magistrates (as clergy) and its emperor (as Christ). Just how far pagan and Christian can be seen to mix in the observances of the Roman Church is a subject of consuming interest to many writers.

The earliest travellers to Rome, if they were not papal legates or merchants, were pilgrims. There is no suggestion that they were interested in the atmosphere or the local customs. They went to see the bones of saints. Handbooks were written for them, and their descriptions of the sights concentrate on the Christian interest, saying nothing about the architecture or the art but listing instead what relics are held by what churches and what martyrs suffered death in which hallowed spots. Sigeric of Glastonbury went to Rome in 990 to receive the pallium, symbol of his investiture as Archbishop of Canterbury, from Pope John XV. His stay there is recorded, though it is nothing like modern travel writing, being merely a catalogue of facts, with no personal reflection or response. We learn that: 'On arriving in Rome, our archbishop went first to the basilica of St Peter the Apostle, then to Santa Maria in Sassia: to San Lorenzo in Lucina: to San Valentino by the Milvian Bridge: to Sant'Agnese: to San Lorenzo fuori le Mura; to San Sebastiano; to Sant'Anastasio: to San Paolo; to San Bonifacio; to Santa Sabina …' and so on. 'Then they went back to their lodging.'

A later handbook, the *Mirabilia Urbis Romae* (*Marvels*

of the City of Rome), written in the mid-12th century and much revised and enlarged after that, tells us about the ancient city too, and the information is disappointingly dull. Of Trajan's Column, for example, we learn that 'The winding pillar of Trajan hath in height one hundred thirty and eight feet, steps in number one hundred fourscore and five, windows forty and five.'

But the *Mirabilia* is not uniformly dry all the way through. Gradually a fondness for anecdote begins to emerge, and with it a tendency to reinterpret history to suit its own interests. Rome, after all, is the centre of the world, the most important city in the universe. All its past greatness cannot have been for nothing; it must stand for Christians and what they believe; its history must have been tending towards what is now held to be right and true. In its telling of the story of Augustus' vision on the Capitoline Hill, pagan and Christian meet and mingle:

On the emperor Augustus' vision of Christ

In the time of the emperor Octavian[1], the Senators, seeing him to be of so great beauty, that none could look into his eyes, and of so great prosperity and peace, that he had made all the world to render him tribute, said unto him: We desire to worship thee, because the godhead is in thee; for it if were not so, all

1 Augustus.

things would not prosper with thee as they do. But he, being loth, demanded a delay, and called unto him the Sibyl of Tibur[2], to whom he rehearsed all that the Senators had said. She begged for three days space, in the which she kept a straight fast; and thus made answer to him after the third day: These things, sir emperor, shall surely come to pass:

Token of doom: the earth shall drip with sweat;
From Heaven shall come the King for evermore,
And present in the flesh shall judge the world.

And anon, whiles Octavian diligently hearkened unto the Sibyl, the heaven was opened, and a great brightness lightened upon him; and he saw in heaven a virgin, passing fair, standing upon an altar, and holding a man-child in her arms, whereof he marvelled exceedingly; and he heard a voice from heaven, saying, This is the altar of the Son of God. The emperor straightway fell to the ground, and worshipped the Christ that should come. This vision he showed to the Senators, and they in like wise marvelled exceedingly. The vision took place in the chamber of the emperor Octavian, where now is the church of Saint Mary in the Capitol. Therefore is it called Saint Mary in ara coeli[3].

Upon another day, when the people had decreed to

2 Tivoli.
3 'Altar of Heaven'.

call him Lord, he forthwith stayed them with hand
and look, neither did he suffer himself to be called
Lord even by his sons, saying: Mortal I am, and will
not call me Lord[4].

From *Mirabilia Urbis Romae*, 12th century,
modern English version by F.M. Nichols, 1889

The church of Santa Maria in Aracoeli on the Capitoline
Hill stands on a numinous spot. Not only was it here
that Augustus had his vision of the Sibyl; here also was
the site of the citadel of the ancient city, where stood a
temple to Juno Moneta, the admonitory goddess, whose
sacred geese set up a honking that warned the Romans
of a Gaulish attack. It was here too that Edward Gibbon
was inspired to write his *Decline and Fall* (*see p. 274*).
The church today possesses a famous and much vener-
ated wooden effigy of a child, the Santissimo Bambino,
which used to be taken to the bedsides of the sick because of its reputedly healing powers. Bernard Berenson, who confessed to 'loving dolls', described it as an
'infant Osiris'. It was stolen in 1994 and never recovered. Today people worship a copy.

At the foot of the Capitoline is the church of San
Giuseppe, more celebrated for what lies beneath it, the
infamous Mamertine Prison. Here religion and supersti-

---

4 Original editor's note: These facts are derived from Suetonius [from his
Lives of the Caesars], and repeated, as having a religious significance.

tion mingle, and pagan history is kept alive in the ghosts of its famous prisoners. Nathaniel Hawthorne visits it and is plainly unsure about its claims to Christian miraculousness, though his scepticism is gentle, that of a Protestant believer rather than an atheist triumphalist.

Nathaniel Hawthorne on the Mamertine Prison

Each visitor was provided with a wax taper, and the *custode* gave one to each of us, bidding us wait a moment while he conducted [a previous group of visitors] to the upper air. During his absence we examined the cell, as well as our dim lights would permit, and soon found an indentation in the wall, with an iron gate put over it for protection, and an inscription above, informing us that the Apostle Peter had left here the imprint of his visage; and, in truth, there is a profile there—forehead, nose, mouth and chin—plainly to be seen, an intaglio in the solid rock. We touched it with the tips of our fingers as well as saw it with our eyes.

The *custode* soon returned, and led us down the darksome steps, chattering in Italian all the time. It is not a very long descent to the lower cell, the roof of which is so low that I believe I could have reached it with my hand. We were now in the deepest and ugliest part of the old Mamertine Prison, one of the few remains of the kingly period of Rome, and which served the Romans as a state prison for hundreds of years before the Christian era. A multitude of criminals or innocent persons, no doubt, have languished here in misery, and perished in darkness. Here Jugurtha starved; here Catiline's adherents were strangled; and methinks, there cannot be in the world such another evil den, so haunted with black memories and indistinct surmises of guilt and suffering. In old Rome, I suppose, the citizens never spoke of this dungeon above their breath. It looks just as bad as it is—round, only seven paces across, yet so obscure that our tapers could not illuminate it from side to side—the stones of which it is constructed being as black as midnight. The *custode* showed us a stone post, at the side of the cell, with the hole in the top of it, into which, he said, St Peter's chain had been fastened; and he uncovered a spring of water, in the middle of the stone floor, which he told us had miraculously gushed up to enable the saint to baptise his jailer. The miracle was perhaps the more easily wrought, inasmuch as Jugurtha had found the floor of the dungeon oozy with wet. However, it is best to be as simple and childlike as we can in these matters; and whether St Peter stamped his visage into the stone, and wrought this other miracle or no, and whether or no he was ever in the prison at all, still the belief of a thousand years and more gives a sort of reality and substance to such traditions. The *custode* dipped an iron ladle into the miraculous water, and we each of us drank a sip; and what is very remarkable to me, it seemed hard water, and almost brackish, while many persons think it the sweetest in Rome. I suspect that St Peter still dabbles in this water, and tempers its qualities according to the faith of those who drink it.

From the *French-Italian Notebooks*, 1872

RELUCTANT CHRISTIANS

Not all visitors to Rome, of course, have been believers. Shelley was an outspoken atheist; indeed, he was assaulted in Rome by a gentleman who was affronted by this outspokenness. It happened on 5th May 1819, when Shelley had gone to collect his letters from the poste-restante office. A 'tall stranger' is said to have gone up to him demanding 'What, are you that damned atheist Shelley?' and knocked him to the floor. Here is Shelley's opinion of the emperor Constantine, whose reign, he believes, exalted a religion directly responsible for a decline in the arts and for the descent from the sunlit uplands of liberal polytheism into the murky depths of the repressive early Church:

Shelley on the Arch of Constantine

Near [the Colosseum] is the arch of Constantine, or rather the arch of Trajan; for the servile and avaricious senate of degraded Rome ordered that the monument of his predecessor should be demolished in order to dedicate one to the Christian reptile, who had crept among the blood of his murdered family to the supreme power. It is exquisitely beautiful and perfect.

Letter to Peacock, 22nd December 1818

In a later letter to the same recipient, Shelley describes the arch again, in similar terms but more insistently: 'The relief and sculpture, and even the colossal images of Dacian captives, were torn by a decree of the senate from an arch dedicated to the latter [Trajan], to adorn that of this stupid and wicked monster, Constantine, one of whose chief merits consists in establishing a religion, the destroyer of those arts which would have rendered so base a spoliation unnecessary. It is an admirable work of art.'

Shelley's attitude set a trend which later developed into the aesthetic movement of the 19th century, whose adherents liked to scorn Christianity and laud the pagan religion, because pagan rituals, being more colourful and voluptuous, correspond better to an aesthete's idea of beauty. In his *Hymn to Proserpine*, Swinburne regrets the passing of the old order and refuses to relinquish his adherence to the old gods, preferring to sink into death in the bosom of his goddess. The new religion is portrayed as poor and mean compared to the sensuous beauty and richness of the old, and the poet predicts that its reign will not last:

Swinburne laments the death of paganism

Though the feet of thine high priests tread where thy
lords and our forefathers trod,

Though these that were Gods are dead, and thou being
dead art a God,

Though before thee the throned Cytherean[5] be fallen,
and hidden her head,

Yet thy kingdom shall pass, Galilean[6], thy dead shall
go down to thee dead.

Of the maiden thy mother men sing as a goddess with
grace clad around;

Thou art throned where another was king; where another
was queen she is crowned.

Yea, once we had sight of another: but now she is
queen, say these.

Not as thine, not as thine was our mother, a blossom
of flowering seas,

Clothed round with the world's desire as with raiment,
and fair as the foam,

And fleeter than kindled fire, and a goddess, and
mother of Rome.

For thine came pale and a maiden, and sister to
sorrow; but ours,

Her deep hair heavily laden with odour and
colour of flowers,

5 Venus.
6 Jesus Christ.

White rose of the rose-white water, a silver
                    splendour, a flame,
Bent down unto us that besought her, and earth grew
                    sweet with her name.
For thine came weeping, a slave among slaves, and
                    rejected; but she
Came flushed from the full-flushed wave, and imperial,
                    her foot on the sea.
And the wonderful waters knew her, the winds and
                    the viewless ways,
And the roses grew rosier, and bluer the sea-blue
                    stream of the bays.
Ye are fallen, our lords, by what token? We wist that ye
                    should not fall.
Ye were all so fair that are broken; and one more
                    fair than ye all.
But I turn to her still, having seen she shall surely
                    abide in the end;
Goddess and maiden and queen, be near me now
                    and befriend.
O daughter of earth, of my mother, her crown and
                    blossom of birth,
I am also, I also, thy brother; I go as I came unto earth.
            From the *Hymn to Prosperine: After the*
    Proclamation in Rome of the Christian Faith, 1866

But the love of artists and aesthetes for paganism is
perhaps unsurprising if Renaissance Rome was, as the

German historian Gregorovius would have us believe, essentially pagan:

Gregorovius on the paganism of Renaissance Rome

In Leo's age[7] paganism seemed entirely to discard the vesture of Christianity...Could a Roman of Cicero's time have been present in the sixteenth century at the festival of one of the saints of the church on whom the epithet of *Divus* had been bestowed, he would scarcely have discovered anything unfamiliar in his surroundings. In Roman sepulchral inscriptions God is again Jupiter...The cardinals were called senators, the saints simply gods (*dii* and *deae*), and the deifying title of *Divus*, as that of *Optimus Maximus*, is usually bestowed on the popes. When Leo ascended the throne the poet Janus Vitalis announced that Jupiter had again descended from Olympus to Rome, and that Leo Medici as Apollo would cure all the maladies of the time. Neither had Julius II been dismayed when one Good Friday a preacher had likened him to Zeus, and compared Christ to Decius or Curtius...On [Leo X's] death the Romans even ventured publicly to sacrifice a bull in the Colosseum to the hostile gods.

Paganism oozed through every pore of Catholicism, in the form of art and religion, of Platonic philosophy and Ciceronian eloquence. Under the hands of Bem-

---

7 Pope Leo X (Giovanni de' Medici, ruled 1513–21).

bo and Sadoleto[8] even the papal bulls adopted the
style and phrases of antiquity. Among the Latins the
Christian religion had become petrified into a pagan
service of the senses and of formulas…From the Platonic school at Florence, which was dissolved in the
beginning of the sixteenth century, issued theistic and
pantheistic ideas, but no definite rationalism. From
this Platonism Italian art erected an ideal enthusiasm
for the Beautiful, and this was its most living influence; it took the place of religion in the Renaissance;
Plato became the apostle of the Beautiful. The sight of
the unutterably depraved priesthood, or the knowledge that the papal power made the greatness of Italy
impossible, may have driven patriotic thinkers such
as Machiavelli to unbelief, while the influence of the
ancient philosophy possibly filled others with con-
tempt for the doctrines of the church…

Sceptics appeared in the liberal schools of Bologna
and Padua who denied the existence of a heaven beyond, while astrology, in affirming the influences of
nativity, destroyed belief in the freedom of will. The
celebrated head of the Italian sceptics was the Man-
tuan Pietro Pomponazzo, and from his school issued
the most renowned scholars of the time. Although in
1513 the Lateran Council found it necessary to pro-

8 Pietro Bembo and Jacopo Sadoleto, distinguished humanist scholars who
both served as secretary to Pope Leo X.

claim belief in the immortality of the soul as an article of faith, Pomponazzo in one of his writings ventured to assert that it was impossible to give rational demonstration of this doctrine, and that it had never been maintained by Aristotle. Thirty years later Pomponazzo would have been burnt for this assertion, but he was now merely punished with censures...

In his youth Leo X had been initiated in debates on Plato's doctrines on the soul; it is said that as pope he once praised the acute arguments with which an opponent of the theory of immortality defended his views; and even if this and other sneers, attributed to Leo and his friends, at 'the profitable fable of Christianity', be untrue, they serve at all events to show the atmosphere that prevailed in the Vatican.

From *The History of the City of Rome in the Middle Ages*, 1859–72, Tr. Mrs G.W. Hamilton

MARTYRDOM, DEVOTION, SACRIFICE

In AD 64, under the emperor Nero, a great fire devastated Rome. In its aftermath, perhaps in a move to turn them into scapegoats, many Christians were horribly executed and there followed a large-scale persecution. Among the victims were St Peter, crucified upside down close to where St Peter's basilica stands today, and St Paul, beheaded at a place between Rome and its port of Ostia. The historian Tacitus would have been about eight years old at the time of the fire. His description shows how the killing of the Christians failed to ignite pure glee among pagan Romans: in fact, the Christians were seen as innocent victims. The poet John Milton, writing many centuries later, is in no doubt that this victimhood will lead to ultimate victory. Charles Burney describes a different kind of victim:

Tacitus on the burning of Rome

It had its beginning in that part of the circus which adjoins the Palatine and Caelian hills, where, amid the shops containing inflammable wares, the conflagration both broke out and instantly became so fierce and so rapid from the wind that it seized in its grasp the entire length of the circus. For here there were no houses fenced in by solid masonry, or temples surrounded by walls, or any other obstacle to interpose delay. The blaze in its fury ran first through the level portions of the city, then rising to the hills, while it again devastated every place below them, it outstripped all preventive measures; so rapid was the mischief and so completely at its mercy the city, with those narrow winding passages and irregular streets, which characterised old Rome. Added to this were the wailings of terror-stricken women, the feebleness of age, the helpless inexperience of childhood, the crowds who sought to save themselves or others, dragging out the infirm or waiting for them, and by their hurry in the one case, by their delay in the other, aggravating the confusion…And no one dared to stop the mischief, because of incessant menaces from a number of persons who forbade the extinguishing of the flames, because again others openly hurled brands, and kept shouting that there was one who gave them authority, either seeking to plunder more freely, or obeying orders.

Nero at this time was at Antium, and did not return to Rome until the fire approached his house, which he had built to connect the palace with the gardens of Maecenas. It could not, however, be stopped from devouring the palace, the house, and everything around it. However, to relieve the people, driven out homeless as they were, he threw open to them the Campus Martius and the public buildings of Agrippa, and even his own gardens, and raised temporary structures to receive the destitute multitude. Supplies of food were brought up from Ostia and the neighbouring towns, and the price of corn was reduced to three sesterces a peck. These acts, though popular, produced no effect, since a rumour had gone forth everywhere that, at the very time when the city was in flames, the emperor appeared on a private stage and sang of the destruction of Troy, comparing present misfortunes with the calamities of antiquity.

At last, after five days, an end was put to the con-

flagration at the foot of the Esquiline hill, by the destruction of all buildings on a vast space, so that the
violence of the fire was met by clear ground and an
open sky. But before people had laid aside their fears,
the flames returned, with no less fury this second
time, and especially in the spacious districts of the
city. Consequently, though there was less loss of life,
the temples of the gods, and the porticoes which were
devoted to enjoyment, fell in a yet more widespread
ruin...Rome, indeed, is divided into fourteen districts, four of which remained uninjured, three were
levelled to the ground, while in the other seven were
left only a few shattered, half-burnt relics of houses...

Nero meanwhile availed himself of his country's
desolation, and erected a mansion[9] in which the jewels and gold, long familiar objects, quite vulgarised
by our extravagance, were not so marvellous as the
fields and lakes, with woods on one side to resemble a
wilderness, and, on the other, open spaces and extensive views...Of Rome meanwhile, so much as was left
unoccupied by his mansion, was not built up, as it
had been after its burning by the Gauls, without any
regularity or in any fashion, but with rows of streets
according to measurement, with broad thoroughfares, with a restriction on the height of houses, with
open spaces, and the further addition of colonnades,

9 The Domus Aurea (*see p. 78*).

as a protection to the frontage of the blocks of tene-
ments…The buildings themselves, to a certain height,
were to be solidly constructed, without wooden
beams, of stone from Gabii or Alba, that material being impervious to fire. And to provide that the water
which individual license had illegally appropriated,
might flow in greater abundance in several places for
the public use, officers were appointed, and everyone
was to have in the open court the means of stopping
a fire. Every building, too, was to be enclosed by its
own proper wall, not by one common to others…

Such indeed were the precautions of human wisdom. The next thing was to seek means of propitiat-
ing the gods, and recourse was had to the Sibylline
books, by the direction of which prayers were offered
to Vulcanus, Ceres, and Proserpina. Juno, too, was
entreated by the matrons…But all human efforts, all
the lavish gifts of the emperor, and the propitiations
of the gods, did not banish the sinister belief that the
conflagration was the result of an order. Consequently, to get rid of the report, Nero fastened the guilt
and inflicted the most exquisite tortures on a class
hated for their abominations, called Christians by
the populace. Christus, from whom the name had its
origin, suffered the extreme penalty during the reign
of Tiberius at the hands of one of our procurators,
Pontius Pilatus, and a most mischievous superstition,
thus checked for the moment, again broke out not

only in Judaea, the first source of the evil, but even in Rome, where all things hideous and shameful from every part of the world find their centre and become popular. Accordingly, an arrest was first made of all who pleaded guilty; then, upon their information, an immense multitude was convicted, not so much of the crime of firing the city, as of hatred against mankind. Mockery of every sort was added to their deaths. Covered with the skins of beasts, they were torn by dogs and perished, or were nailed to crosses, or were doomed to the flames and burnt, to serve as a nightly illumination, when daylight had expired.

Nero offered his gardens for the spectacle, and was exhibiting a show in the circus, while he mingled with the people in the dress of a charioteer or stood aloft on a car. Hence, even for criminals who deserved extreme and exemplary punishment, there arose a feeling of compassion; for it was not, as it seemed, for the public good, but to glut one man's cruelty, that they were being destroyed.

> From the *Annals*, Book XV, 2nd century AD,
> Tr. A.J. Church and W.J. Brodribb

John Milton champions Christianity

In Book IV of *Paradise Regained*, Satan tempts Christ by presenting a view of Rome to him though his 'aerie microscope', as if in a camera obscura. Tiberius is on the throne, but he is elderly and depraved. The Empire is up for grabs, if only a strong man would take it… No, says Christ (who was crucified in the reign of Tiberius), it is not thus that I shall come into my own:

And now the Tempter thus his silence broke.
  'The city which thou seest no other deem
Than great and glorious Rome, Queen of the Earth
So far renowned, and with the spoils enriched
Of nations. There the Capitol thou seest,
Above the rest lifting his stately head
On the Tarpeian rock, her citadel
Impregnable; and there Mount Palatine,
The imperial palace, compass huge, and high
The structure, skill of noblest architects,
With gilded battlements, conspicuous far,
Turrets, and terraces, and glittering spires.
Many a fair edifice besides, more like
Houses of gods (so well I have disposed
My Aerie Microscope) thou may'st behold,
Outside and inside both, pillars and roofs
Carv'd work, the hand of famed artificers
In cedar, marble, ivory, or gold.
Thence to the gates cast round thine eye, and see
What conflux issuing forth, or entering in:
Praetors, proconsuls to their provinces
Hasting, or on return, in robes of state;
Lictors and rods, the ensigns of their power;
Legions and cohorts, turms of horse and wings;

Or embassies from regions far remote,
In various habits…
All nations now to Rome obedience pay—
To Rome's great Emperor…
This Emperor[10] hath no son, and now is old,
Old and lascivious, and from Rome retired
To Capreae, an island small but strong
On the Campanian shore, with purpose there
His horrid lusts in private to enjoy;
Committing to a wicked favourite
All public cares, and yet of him suspicious;
Hated of all, and hating. With what ease,
Endued with regal virtues as thou art,
Appearing, and beginning noble deeds,
Might'st thou expel this monster from his throne,
Now made a sty, and, in his place ascending,
A victor-people free from servile yoke!
And with my help thou may'st…'

To whom the Son of God, unmoved, replied:—
'Nor doth this grandeur and majestic shew
Of luxury, though called magnificence,
More than of arms before, allure mine eye,
Much less my mind; though thou should'st add to tell
Their sumptuous gluttonies, and gorgeous feasts
On citron tables or Atlantic stone

10 Tiberius retired to Capri leaving Caligula in charge.

…Then embassies thou shew'st
From nations far and nigh! What honour that,
But tedious waste of time, to sit and hear
So many hollow compliments and lies,
Outlandish flatteries? Then proceed'st to talk
Of the Emperor, how easily subdued,
How gloriously I shall, thou say'st, expel
A brutish monster: what if I withal
Expel a Devil who first made him such?
Let his tormentor, Conscience, find him out;
For him I was not sent, nor yet to free
That people, victor once, now vile and base,
Deservedly made vassal—who, once just,
Frugal and mild, and temperate, conquered well,
But govern ill the nations under yoke,
Peeling their provinces, exhausted all
By lust and rapine; first ambitious grown
Of triumph, that insulting vanity;
Then cruel, by their sports to blood inured
Of fighting beasts, and men to beasts exposed;
Luxurious by their wealth, and greedier still,
And from the daily Scene effeminate.
What wise and valiant man would seek to free
These, thus degenerate, by themselves enslaved,
Or could of inward slaves make outward free?
Know, therefore, when my season comes to sit
On David's throne, it shall be like a tree
Spreading and overshadowing all the earth,

Or as a stone that shall to pieces dash
All monarchies besides throughout the world;
And of my Kingdom there shall be no end.'
From *Paradise Regained*, Book IV, 1671

Charles Burney sees a nun take the veil

This morning I went to the convent of St Ursula, to
see a nun take the veil…I was placed close to the altar, where I could see the whole ceremony, and hear
every word that was uttered. The service was begun
by saying Mass; then Cardinal Rossi entered in great
state, while the organ was playing and the Mass was
singing: the music, both vocal and instrumental, was
performed by the nuns and ladies of the convent,
who were placed in the organ gallery. The composition was pretty, but ill-executed; the organ was a bad
one, and too powerful for the band.

When the Cardinal was robed, the novitiate was…
brought to the altar in exceedingly high dress. Her
hair was of a beautiful light brown, and curled *en tête
de mouton* all over her head. Her gown was of the richest embroidery, and, I believe, embossed, blue and
silver, I ever saw. She had on a large stage hoop, and
a great quantity of diamonds; the train of her robe
dragged full two yards on the ground; she seemed
rather a pretty sort of young person than a great
beauty. When she first appeared, she looked very
pale, and more dead than alive; she made a most pro-

found reverence to the Cardinal, who was seated on the steps of the altar in his mitre and all his rich vestments, ready to receive her. She threw herself upon her knees at the foot of the altar, and remained in that posture some time, while other parts of the ceremony were adjusting; then she walked up to the Cardinal. 'My child, what is your request?' She said that she begged to be admitted into the convent as a sister of the order of St Ursula. 'Have you well,' said the Cardinal, 'considered what you ask?' She answered, cheerfully, that she had, and was well informed of all she was about to do. Then she kneeled down again, and kissed the Cardinal's hands, and received from him a little Crucifix, which she also kissed…After this there was a sermon in the Italian language, and that being over, the Cardinal led the nun-elect into the convent, where she was divested of all her gorgeous attire and worldly vanities, and had her hair cut off. She then came to the gate in her religious dress, to receive the white veil, with which she was invested by the lady abbess…After this there was more pretty music badly performed. The organ, by executing all the symphonies and accompaniments, overpowered the violins, and had a bad effect, though neatly played…

When her veil was on, the new sister came to the convent door to receive the congratulations of her friends and of the company; but first, with a lighted taper in her hand, she went round the convent to salute all the nuns, who had likewise tapers in their hands…At the altar she changed countenance several times, first pale, then red, and seemed to pant, and to be in danger of either bursting into tears or fainting; but she recovered before the ceremony was ended, and at the convent door assumed an air of great cheerfulness; talked to several of her friends and acquaintance, and seemed to give up the world very heroically. And thus ended this human sacrifice!

From *The Present State of Music in France and Italy*, 1773

THE CULT OF REPUBLICANISM

A large body of people, particularly in the late 18th and early 19th centuries, were attracted to Rome by a different creed: Republicanism. Just as the Catholic Church was keen to point out a continuity between pagan Rome with its sibyls and emperors and Christianity with its prophets and popes (both emperor and pope were styled *Pontifex Maximus*: chief bridge-builder between human and divine), so too were republicans keen to demonstrate a living tradition of Roman democracy. But there were not many monuments of the Roman Republic to be found in the city. Still fewer then, when much less had been excavated. John Cam Hobhouse, the friend and annotator of Byron, writes in disgruntled vein, of the difficulty in finding anything in Rome that is a true survival from the days of the early Republic, without the admixture and contamination of the Empire:

Hobhouse on the lack of republican monuments

It is not to worship at the shrine of the Flavian princes nor to do homage to the forbearance of Trajan, or to the philosophy of Aurelius[11] that we undertake the pilgrimage of Rome. The men whose traces we would wish to discover were cast in another mould, and belonged to that order of beings whose superior qualities were by the wisest of their immediate successors as well as by the slaves of the last emperors, acknowledged to have expired with the republic. It is with the builders, and not the dilapidators of the Roman race that we would hope to meet in the Capitol. Our youthful pursuits inspire us with no respect or affection for this nation independent of their republican virtues. It is to refresh our recollections of those virtues that we explore the ruins of the city which gave them birth; and absorbed by an early devotion for the patriots of Rome, we are indifferent to the records of her princes. We feel no sympathy with the survivors of Philippi[12]. We would prefer a single fragment of

11 Marcus Aurelius (ruled 121–80), author of the *Meditations*.
12 The survivors of Philippi are Augustus and Mark Antony, who defeated the armies of Caesar's assassins Brutus and Cassius.

the Palatine house of Hortensius or of Cicero[13] to all
the lofty ruins which fringe the imperial hill.

As it is, we must visit a sepulchre or a museum;
must trust to one amongst a range of doubtful busts;
must unravel an inscription, and extricate ourselves
from antiquarian doubts before we are recalled to the
city of the Scipios, whilst everything around us attests
the might and the magnificence of the Caesars.

From the *Historical Illustrations of the Fourth*
Canto of 'Childe Harold', 1818

EASTERN CULTS IN ANCIENT ROME

Rome did not set out to be tolerant of the gods of its conquered peoples. However, as the Empire expanded and
there were more and more people to be accommodated
peaceably, it found it expedient to admit them. The most
popular were the so-called mystery cults—of Persian
Mithras, Egyptian Isis and Hebrew Jesus—all of which
contained the idea of hope for an afterlife and were concerned with notions of perfectibility and redemption,
and of striving from darkness into light. Not surpris-
ingly, given their earthly lives of harsh discipline, op-
pression and servitude, the people who were especially
drawn to such cults were soldiers, women and slaves.

---

13 Hortensius, like Cicero, was an orator of the late Republic.

For Gibbon, in *Decline and Fall*, the co-existence of these cults[14] is a major cause of 'the union and internal prosperity' of the Empire. A contemporary story of initiation into the Egyptian cult of Osiris is given by Apuleius.

Gibbon on religious tolerance in ancient Rome

It is not alone by the rapidity or extent of conquest that we should estimate the greatness of Rome. The sovereign of the Russian deserts commands a larger portion of the globe. In the seventh summer after his passage of the Hellespont, Alexander erected the Macedonian trophies on the banks of the Hyphasis. Within less than a century, the irrepressible Zingis, and the Mogul princes of his race, spread their cruel devastations and transient empire from the sea of China to the confines of Egypt and Germany. But the firm edifice of Roman power was raised and preserved by the wisdom of ages. The obedient provinces of Trajan and the Antonines were united by laws and adorned by arts. They might occasionally suffer from the partial abuse of delegated authority; but the general principle of government was wise, simple and beneficent. They enjoyed the religion of their ancestors, whilst in civil honours and advantages they were exalted, by just degrees, to an equality with their conquerors.

The policy of the emperors and the senate, as far as

14 NB: Women were not drawn to Mithraism; it excluded them.

it concerned religion, was happily seconded by the
reflections of the enlightened and by the habits of the
superstitious part of their subjects. The various modes
of worship which prevailed in the Roman world were
all considered by the people as equally true; by the
philosopher as equally false; and by the magistrate as
equally useful. And thus toleration produced not only
mutual indulgence, but even religious concord.

The superstition of the people was not embittered
by any mixture of theological rancour; nor was it
confined by the chains of any speculative system. The
devout polytheist, though fondly attached to his national rites, admitted with implicit faith the different
religions of the earth.

From *The History of the Decline and Fall
of the Roman Empire*, 1776–89

Apuleius becomes a proselyte of Osiris

Apuleius' *Metamorphoses*, popularly known as *The Gold-
en Ass*, the only Latin 'novel' to survive in its entirety,
is the picaresque tale of a man who experiments with
magic and ends up turning himself into a donkey. After
many adventures he is saved by the goddess Isis, sister
and wife of Osiris, whose devotee he becomes at Rome:

I made up my packet, and took shipping toward
the City of Rome, where with a prosperous wind I
arrived about the 12th day of December. And the

greatest desire that I had there was daily to make my prayers to the sovereign goddess Isis, who by reason of the place where her temple was builded, was called Campensis[15], and continually adored of the people of Rome. Her minister and worshipper was I, howbeit I was a stranger to her Church, and unknown to her religion there.

When the year was ended, and the goddess warned me again to receive this new order and consecration, I marvelled greatly what it should signify, and what should happen, considering that I was a sacred person already. But it fortuned that while I partly reasoned with myself, and partly examining the thing with the priests and bishops, there came a new and marvellous thought in my mind: that is to say, I was *only religious to the goddess Isis*, but not sacred to the religion of great Osiris, the sovereign father of all the goddesses, between whom, although there was a religious unity and concord, yet there was a great difference of order and ceremony. And because it was necessary that I should likewise be a minister unto Osiris, there was no long delay: for in the night after, there appeared unto me one of that order, covered with linen robes, holding in his hands spears wrapped in ivy, and other things

15 The Temple of Isis was built on the Field of Mars (Campus Martius) and was known as the Isaeum Campensis.

not convenient to declare, which then he left in my
chamber, and sitting in my seat, recited to me such
things as were necessary for the sumptuous banquet
of mine entry. And [so that] I might know him again,
he showed me how the ankle of his left foot was
somewhat maimed, which caused him a little to halt.

After [having manifestly discovered] the will of the
god Osiris, when matins was ended, I went from one
to another to find him out which had the halting
mark on his foot, according as I learned by my vision. At length I found it true: for I perceived one
of the company of the priests who had not only the
token of his foot, but the stature and habit of his
body resembling in every point as he appeared in
the night: he was called Asinius Marcellus, a name
not much disagreeing from my transformation[16].
By and by I went to him, which knew well enough
all the matter, as being admonished by like precept
in the night: for the night before, as he dressed the
flowers and garlands about the head of the god Osiris, he understood by the mouth of the image which
told the predestinations of all men, how he had sent
a poor man of Madura[17] to whom he should minister
his sacraments, [so that] he should receive a reward
by divine providence, and the other glory for his

16 The Latin word for ass is *asinus*.
17 A town in Roman Numidia, now M'Daourouch, Algeria.

virtuous studies. When I saw my self thus deputed unto religion, my desire was stopped by reason of poverty, for I had spent a great part of my goods in travel and peregrination, but most of all in the City of Rome, whereby my low estate withdrew me a great while.

In the end being oft times stirred forward, not without great trouble of mind, I was constrained to sell my robe for a little money, howbeit sufficient for all my affairs. Then the priest spake unto me saying, 'How is it that for a little pleasure thou art not afraid to sell thy vestments, and entering into so great ceremonies, fearest to fall into poverty? Prepare thyself, and abstain from all animal meats, [both] beasts and fish.' In the mean season I frequented the sacrifices of Serapis, which were done in the night, which thing gave me great comfort to my peregrination, and ministered unto me more plentiful living, considering I gained some money in haunting the court, by reason of my Latin tongue.

From *Metamorphoses* or *The Golden Ass*,
2nd century AD, Tr. William Adlington, 1566

PAPAL ROME & ST PETER'S

'We declare, we proclaim, we define that it is absolutely nec-essary for salvation that every human creature be subject to the Roman Pontiff.'   Bull of Pope Boniface VIII, 1302

Today the Vatican is a tiny sovereign state of under half a square kilometre; but when many of the travellers quoted in this book went there it was the residence, in his capital city, of a temporal monarch. The pope was not only the supreme pontiff, Bishop of Rome and vicar of Christ on earth, but he was also lord of the Papal States, the lands of St Peter, whose territory had once stretched from Ancona on the Adriatic all the way across the centre of Italy to its capital at Rome. Rome remained loyal to the papacy until 1870, when the forces of Pope Pius IX were finally defeated and the city joined the Kingdom of Italy. Until this date, many writers indulged in right-eous indignation at the tyranny of papal rule: spiritual fathers-turned-secular emperors were an easy target for political mockery—but those same writers also enjoyed the picturesqueness that papal power brought with it, the prelates in their sedan chairs on the Pincian Hill, the subject people in their poetic servitude. And the pope himself was a celebrity. The same *New York Times* correspondent who was so horrified by the quantities of goat droppings in the streets (*see p. 19*) also meets Pope Pius IX, and is beside himself with excitement:

The New York Times meets the pope

Who comes to Rome without seeing the Pope? I met him the other day on the Via Angelica, a pleasant, shady street that runs out north under the walls of the Vatican, where he had gone, as is his wont, to take an evening drive. He generally drives out between 5 and 6 o'clock, goes out a few hundred rods and then dismounts and walks. I saw him walk over a mile, and then he disappeared from sight still walking, while his carriage followed slowly on behind. He walks with the totter peculiar to old age and with a considerable stoop, and yet with not a little rapidity and energy. I am bound to say PIUS IX has the pleasantest face I have seen in Europe; his good nature amounts to a weakness, and his hesitation is said to give his councilors much trouble.   18th May 1867

Frederick Rolfe imagines becoming pope

The protagonist of Rolfe's strange novel *Hadrian the Seventh* is George Rose, a thinly-disguised alter ego of the author. He is portrayed, in Rolfe's idiosyncratic prose, as a misfit, despised and rejected by men, who is providentially given the chance to show the world what it has been missing. Elected pope, he takes the regnal name of

Hadrian, which had been the name of the only English pope, Nicholas Breakspear, who reigned as Hadrian IV from 1154 to 1159. The scene opens in St Peter's Square:

A tiny figure splashed a web of cloth-of-gold over the balcony; and a tiny ermine and vermilion figure ascended, placing a tiny triple cross. Came in a stentorian megaphonic roar a proclamation by the Cardinal-Archdeacon,

'I announce to you great joy. We have for a Pope the Lord George of the Roses of England, Who has imposed upon himself the name of Hadrian the Seventh.

He gave place to another tiny figure, silver and gold, irradiant in the sun. A clear thin thread of a voice sang,

'Our help is in the name of the Lord.'

Phonographs recorded the sonorous response,

'Who hath made heaven and earth.'

Hadrian the Seventh raised His hand and sang again,

'May Almighty God, Father, Son, and Holy Ghost, bless you.'

It was the Apostolic Benediction of the City and the World.

Now things went briskly. There was a brain which schemed and a will to be obeyed. The hands began to realize that they would have to act manually. Dear deliberate Rome simply gasped at a Pontiff who said 'To-

morrow' and meant it. The Sacred College found that
it had no option. Naturally it looked as black as night.
But the Cardinal-Archdeacon could not refuse point-
blank to crown; and, when Hadrian announced that
His incoronation would take place in the morning on
the steps of St Peter's, futile effort suggested difficulty
preventing possibility. That was the only course open
to the opposition. Three cardinals in turn announced
that there would not be time to give notice of the
ceremony, to arrange the church, to issue tickets of
admission. Another courted catastrophe saying that
there was no time to summon the proper officials.
He heard that there were sixteen hours in which to
summon those who actually were indispensable. A
fifth said that, owing to the antichristian tendencies
of the times, no representatives of the King of France,
of the Holy Roman Emperor, of the First Conservator of the Roman people, were forthcoming; and he
politely inquired how the quadruplex lavation could
be performed in their absence? The Pope responded
that He was capable of washing His hands four times
without any assistance, in the absence of legitimate
assistants: but the General of the Church was not to
seek: the modern Syndic of Rome was the equivalent
of the ancient First Conservator: the Austrian Ambassador could represent the Empire: while, as for
wretched kingless unkingly France—let someone instantly go out into the streets of Rome and catch the

first Christian Frenchman there encountered. Any-
how, the quadruplex lavation was accidental. The
essential was that the Supreme Pontiff should sing
a pontifical mass at the high altar of St Peter's, and
should receive the triple crown. These things would
be done at eight o'clock on the following morning.
All the doors of the basilica were to be fixed open
at midnight; and so remain. No official notice need
be published. And that was all. Then the Pope shut
up Himself in His predecessor's gorgeous rooms, inspecting them till they gave him a pain in His eyes.
Luckily He had secured his pouch-full of tobacco and
a book of cigarette-papers: He smoked, and thought,
looking out of the windows over Rome.

From Hadrian the Seventh, 1904

Montaigne witnesses an excommunication

On the morning of Holy Thursday the pope, attired
in pontificals, appeared under the first portico of St
Peter's, on the second floor, accompanied by his cardinals, and carrying a torch in his hand. There, on
one side, a canon of St Peter's read out a Latin bull in
which an infinite variety of people were excommuni-
cated, among them the Huguenots…and any prince
who had holdings in some way encroaching on
Church lands—at which clause the cardinals Medici
and Carafa, who were with the pope, chuckled exceedingly. The reading of the bull lasted a good hour

and a half; for after each clause, which the canon read in Latin, the Cardinal Gonzaga, from the other side, gave an Italian translation. After this the pope threw the lighted torch down to the people…It fell among them and there was all the trouble in the world about getting a scrap of it, and people were pummelling each other fiercely with fists and staves. While the condemnation was being read out, there was a large piece of black taffeta draped over the balcony of the said portico, in front of the pope. Once the excommunications were done, this black hanging was removed, revealing another in a different colour: now the pope pronounced his public benedictions.

From the *Journal de Voyage*, 1581 (Tr. AB)

ST PETER'S

One of the best portraits of the Vatican, and its great basilica of St Peter, is painted by the German historian Ferdinand Gregorovius. In St Peter's are housed four major relics, beneath the great dome of Michelangelo. These are the bones of St Andrew; the lance of St Longinus, which pierced the side of Christ on the Cross; a fragment of the True Cross; and the veil of St Veronica, the cloth with which she is said to have mopped the Saviour's brow on his way to Calvary. Thereby hangs the following tale:

Gregorovius on the relic of St Veronica

Tiberius, afflicted with incurable leprosy, one day informed the senators that, being beyond the aid of man, he must have recourse to heaven. He had been told that a divine magician, named Jesus, dwelt in Jerusalem, and he ordered the patrician Volusianus immediately to repair thither and implore the renowned physician to accompany him back to the Imperial court. Storms delayed the arrival of the messenger for a whole year; and on reaching Jerusalem, Volusian was met by Pilate with regrets that the Emperor had not sooner made known his desires, as the magician had already been crucified…Volusian, unable to execute his commission, thought himself fortunate in obtaining a portrait of Jesus. Veronica, a pious matron, had wiped the face of the Saviour as he passed, overpowered by the weight of the cross, and the Saviour, in return, had allowed the cloth to retain the impress of His features. Volusian conducted Veronica, and with her the portrait, back to Rome, bringing Pilate in chains on board the same vessel. When they arrived in the presence of the Emperor, Tiberius sentenced the ex-governor to life-long exile…The handkerchief he ordered to be brought before him, and hardly had he set eyes on it when he…fell on his knees in adoration, and immediately recovered of his leprosy.

From *The History of the City of Rome in the Middle Ages*, 1859–72, Tr. Mrs G.W. Hamilton

Visitors' reactions to the architecture of St Peter's have been mixed. Wordsworth loved it. 'Though I have seen the Coliseum, the Pantheon, and all the other boasted things,' he wrote in 1837, 'nothing has in the least approached the impressions I received from the inside of St Peter's.' The poet and historian Macaulay, writing a year later, said simply, 'I never in my life saw, and never, I suppose, shall I again see, anything so astonishingly beautiful.' Shelley was less impressed, pronouncing that 'Internally it exhibits littleness on a large scale, and is in every respect opposed to antique taste'. Gregorovius complained of its lack of mystery: 'In the interior the masses of the piers, the arches and barrel-vaulting suggest immensity but not infinity...In St Peter's the language of religion is translated into the modern, secular and profane style of a period of soulless splendour.'

While J.B.S. Morritt loved Bernini's colonnade in front ('No church equals it approach'), he objected to the architectural ground-plan: 'In the front there are great architectural blunders,' he says, 'and the miserable superstition of its forming a cross has fettered the noblest plan ever conceived to man, and induced in many instances a departure from the designs of Michael Angelo whose idea was to have shortened the middle aisle and to have made it a grand portico, with the dome rising over it.' Ruskin doesn't beat about the bush. He hated it, as the extracts below show, both of them written in the full flush of adolescent arrogance:

Ruskin rubbishes St Peter's

St Peter's I expected to be *disappointed* in. I was *disgusted*. The Italians think Gothic architecture barbarous. I think Greek heathenish. Greek, by-the-bye, it is not, but it has all its weight and clumsiness without its dignity or simplicity. As a whole, St Peter's is fit for nothing but a ball-room, and it is a little too gaudy even for that (inside I mean, of course)…As a whole…it is meagre outside and offensive within.

Letter to the Rev. T. Dale, 1840

St Peter's!—Pshaw! I never saw so much good marble and ground wasted. They don't know what architecture means, in Italy; it is all bigness and blaze with them.   *Letter to a college friend*

Thomas Gray was interested in the ritual at St Peter's as well as in the architecture. He was there at the end of Holy Week, on Good Friday, and writes to his mother about what he saw. The Good Friday illuminations were famous, and all visitors went to see them:

Thomas Gray in St Peter's

To-day I am just come from paying my adoration at St Peter's to three extraordinary reliques, which are exposed to public view only on these two days in the whole year, at which time all the confraternities in the city come in procession to see them. It was something extremely novel to see that vast church, the most magnificent in the world, undoubtedly, illuminated (for it was night) by thousands of little crystal lamps, disposed in the figure of a huge cross at the high altar, and seeming to hang alone in the air. All the light proceeded from this, and had the most singular effect imaginable as one entered the great door. Soon after came one after another, I believe, thirty processions, all dressed in linen frocks, and girt with a cord, their heads covered with a cowl all over, only two holes to see through left. Some of them were all black, others red, others white, others party-coloured; these were continually coming and going with their tapers and crucifixes before them; and to each company, as they arrived and knelt before the great altar, were shown from a balcony at a great height, the three wonders, which are, you must know, the head of the spear that wounded Christ; St Veronica's handkerchief, with the miraculous impression of his face upon it; and a piece of the true cross, on the sight of which the people thump their breasts, and kiss the pavement with vast devotion. The tragical part of the ceremony is half a dozen wretched creatures, who with their faces covered, but naked to the waist, are in a side-chapel disciplining themselves with scourges full of iron prickles; but really in earnest, as our eyes can testify, which saw their backs and arms so raw we should have taken it for a red satin doublet torn, and showing the skin through, had we not been convinced to the contrary by the blood with was plentifully sprinkled about them…

Letter to his mother, 15th April, 1740

Barbara Pym on St Peter's

March 1945: St Peter's. Vast and unchurchlike. Marble in various colours. Nice Holy Water basins, white cherubs and yellow Siena marble. It was Palm Sunday and outside they were selling palms and little palm crosses and everyone carried sprigs of myrtle. All the pictures behind the altars were veiled in purple. We went up on the roof—the Tiber a yellowish brown—lovely bridges with figures. Palazzo Venezia looks good in the distance, flying statues on the corners—figures everywhere stand out against the sky. Peered into the Vatican City in the hopes of seeing carpet slippers slopping up and down the backstairs. Hens on the roof.

From *A Very Private Eye: An Autobiography in Diaries and Letters*, 1984

ROME & THE REFORMATION

The Protestant Reformation was one of the most momentous things ever to happen to papal Rome. It shook the city to its foundations, not only through the loss of millions of souls to Protestantism but also in the sense that it shook the Church up. The Counter-Reformation was launched. Nicholas V, the pope who had instigated the sumptuous rebuilding of St Peter's and who had transferred the papal residence from the Lateran Palace to the Vatican, said plainly to his cardinals in his death-bed speech that the general mass of mankind, 'ignorant of letters and wholly untouched by them, lose their belief in the course of time…unless they are moved by certain extraordinary sights.' Years later his words were taken to heart. Churches became more splendid than ever, more theatrical, as they aimed to capture men's hearts and minds, and thereby their souls, by the thrill of spectacle. The greed, arrogance, covetousness, lust and other deadly sins of the priesthood were also curbed, with the institution of new religious orders, a new austerity, and a new terror: the Inquisition.

Two of the greatest figures of the Reformation visited Rome: Erasmus was in the city in 1509 and in many ways liked what he saw; Martin Luther came in 1511, and didn't. Both visits were made during the pontificate of Julius II. In 1520 Julius' successor, Leo X, issued a bull condemning sections of Luther's writings, which Luther famously consigned to the flames at Wittenberg.

Thomas Carlyle on Luther in Rome

It was in his twenty-seventh year that he first saw Rome; being sent thither…on a mission from his

Convent. Pope Julius the Second, and what was going on at Rome, must have filled the mind of Luther
with amazement. He had come as to the Sacred City,
throne of God's High-priest on Earth; and he found
it—what we know! Many thoughts it must have given
the man; many which we have no record of, which
perhaps he did not himself know how to utter. This
Rome, this scene of false priests, clothed not in the
beauty of holiness, but in far other vesture, is false:
but what is it to Luther? A mean man he, how shall
he reform a world? That was far from his thoughts. A
humble, solitary man, why should he at all meddle
with the world? It was the task of quite higher men
than he. His business was to guide his own footsteps
wisely through the world. Let him do his own obscure duty in it well; the rest, horrible and dismal as
it looks, is in God's hand, not in his.

It is curious to reflect what might have been the
issue, had Roman Popery happened to pass this
Luther by...

From *On Heroes and Hero-Worship*, 1869

Gregorovius on Erasmus in Rome

Ferdinand Gregorovius, the great historian of medieval and Renaissance Rome, was a Protestant, and was
naturally interested in Erasmus. He vividly portrays
the double-edged impressions the great humanist must
have taken away with him:

Erasmus fell under the spell of the city...Rome as the theatre of the world and its culture fascinated the greatest scholar of the time. Monuments, art and collections, libraries, the wealth of learning and intellect, the grandiose style of life, all filled him with admiration. As a satirist it seemed to him a great European carnival, where worldly vanity went masked in spiritual attire, where were represented all lusts and desires, all intrigues and crimes, their magnet the Vatican, and thirst for gold, honours and power the forces that moved them...As a Christian he was astonished at the bold and glaring colouring borrowed from paganism by the Roman religion, of which nothing remained that was not false, she whose formerly revered temple had been transformed by the ambition and rapacity of the priesthood into a European banking house and a retail market for diplomas of favours, indulgences and objects of superstition. As a man of the world, however, Erasmus could not feel otherwise than at ease in the courts of cardinals, and above all he had to acknowledge that in this corrupt Rome were found the most liberal form of intercourse and the most exquisite courtesy...The papacy, learning, antiquity, art, all linked Roman society in correspondence with the world...The wealth of intellectual life flourished here in the morass of vice.

From *The History of the City of Rome in the Middle Ages*, 1859–72, Tr. Mrs G.W. Hamilton

In 1514 a scurrilous pamphlet was published anonymously in Latin, with the title *Julius Exclusus e Coelis* (*Julius Debarred from Heaven*). Authorship is still not certain but most scholars believe it to have been written by Erasmus. It takes the form of a dialogue between the lately-dead pontiff, Julius II, and St Peter. Pope Julius arrives drunk at the pearly gates and finds them locked. A debate ensues wherein St Peter asks the pope why he believes he should be admitted. The debate is between the worldly and the spiritual, but it also raises the question of how to present Christian majesty to mortal men. Through military aggression, pomp and splendour, with the pope arrayed as Almighty God, awing the faithful and cowing their enemies? Or with simple humility, with the pope as vicar of Christ, sent to earth to teach men to be meek? Julius is firmly of the former view. His whole pontificate was one of battle and conquest, pomp and ceremony, art and adornment:

Erasmus lampoons the worldliness of popes

[ST] PETER: So far I have heard the words of a secular leader, not a churchman. And not so much secular as pagan—more wicked even than the pagans. You boast of being an expert at rupturing treaties, at fomenting war, at inciting human slaughter. This is the power of Satan, not of a pontiff. Whosoever styles himself Vicar of Christ should endeavour to come as close as he can to His model. In Him, after all, supreme power is allied to supreme good; He has supreme wisdom, but of the simplest kind. In you I see an image of supreme power coupled with supreme evil and supreme crassness. So much so that if the prince of evil, the Devil, wished to appoint himself a vicar, who better to choose but someone like you? In what way have you ever behaved like an apostolic person?

[POPE] JULIUS: What can be more apostolic than enlarging the Church of Christ?

PETER: But if the Church is the Christian people, those conjoined in the spirit of Christ, it appears to me a subversion of the Church to provoke the entire world to dire wars, so that your evil and pestilence might go unpunished.

JULIUS: What we mean by the Church are its sacred buildings, its priests, and in particular the Roman curia, myself most of all, who am the Church's head.

PETER: But Christ made us ministers, with Himself the head—unless a second head has now sprouted. But tell me, in what ways has the Church been enlarged?

JULIUS: Enlarged—you're getting the point at last! That Church, once starving and beggarly, is now blooming, with all manner of embellishments.

PETER: Such as? The zeal of the faithful?

JULIUS: Come off it!

PETER: Holy law?

JULIUS: You're being deliberately obtuse.

PETER: Rejection of the world?

JULIUS: Do I have to spell it out? *Real* embellishments. Those things you mentioned are just bla-bla.

PETER: Very well, so what are these embellishments?

JULIUS: Regal palaces, beautiful horses and mules, fleets of servants, crack troops, splendid retainers…

GUARDIAN ANGEL: Gorgeous whores, complaisant pimps.

JULIUS: …gold, purple, and so much revenue that there's no king on the planet that wouldn't seem humble and poor when compared in wealth and estate with the Pope of Rome; no one so ambitious that he wouldn't own himself outdone; no one so luxurious that he wouldn't curse his own meanness; no one so rich, not even a usurer, that he wouldn't envy our wealth. These are the kind of ornaments I mean, and I have husbanded them and increased them.

PETER: All right. But who was the first, with these so-called 'embellishments', to sully and weigh down the Church which Christ desired to be wholly pure and unencumbered?

JULIUS: What's that got to do with anything? The point is, we have all this; we own it; we enjoy it. You know, there are people who say that some chap called Constantine turned over the whole majesty of his empire to Pope Sylvester, lock, stock and barrel: accoutrements, horses, chariots, helmet, belt and cloak, his retinue, swords, crowns of gold (the very purest gold, by the way), army, siege engines, cities, kingdoms…

PETER: And is there any official record of this largesse?[1]

JULIUS: None. Except for one, mixed up with a load of decretals.

PETER: Perhaps it's all a myth, then.

JULIUS: Funny you should say that, because that's just what I think. After all, who in their right mind would hand over such a magnificent empire, even to his own father? Still, it's a lovely story—and I've always managed to intimidate loud-mouthed doubters into silence.

PETER: So far I've heard nothing from you but worldly concerns.

JULIUS: Could it be that you're still dreaming of the Church as it was in your day? When you and a handful of starveling bishops presided over a chilly, plodding pontificate, always at the mercy of poverty, toil, danger and a thousand other ghastly inconveniences? Things have moved on since then. The Pope of Rome is a far cry now from what he was. You were just pope by name. If only you could see us now, see the sheer number of sacred buildings built with kings' fortunes, the thousands of prelates everywhere—many of them with handsome incomes—the hordes of bishops, all quite the equal of royalty in terms of arms and wealth, the myriad magnificent episcopal palaces—and par-

---

1 Erasmus is alluding to the 'Donation of Constantine', a forged document of the 8th century which was used by the popes to justify their claims to temporal as well as spiritual power.

ticularly in Rome if you could only see the purple cardinals surrounded by their great retinues, the masses of horses (more than a king's train) and mules caparisoned with fine lawn, gold and gems, some even shod in silver and gold. And then if you were to glimpse the Supreme Pontiff, borne aloft by the guard on his throne of gold, motioning with his hand to the faithful as he passes; if you could hear the thundering cannon, the clamour of trumpets, the roar of the crowd and their acclamations; if you could see the blaze of artillery fire, the glitter of the torchlight—and even the most splendid of princes scarcely allowed so much as to kiss the blessed feet; ooh, if you could have seen that Roman priest using his foot to place the crown on the Holy Roman Emperor's head! The Holy Roman Emperor, mind, king of all the world if written laws mean anything (though in fact his fancy title is just a dumbshow). In short, if you'd seen and heard all this, what would you say?

PETER: That I was looking at a tyrant worse than worldly, the enemy of Christ, bane of the Church.

JULIUS: Oh, you'd change your tune if you saw one of my triumphs. Take the one where I entered Bologna or the one I held at Rome after trouncing the Venetians. Or indeed the one where I re-entered Rome after fleeing Bologna. Or what about my most recent one, which I celebrated after thrashing the French at Ravenna, when we had seemed a dead cert to lose?

If you could only have seen the palfreys, the horses, the ranks of armed soldiers, the captains' insignia, the procession of lovely boys, the flaming torches everywhere, the whole grand apparatus, the pomp of the bishops and splendour of the cardinals, the trophies, the spoils, the shouts of the people and soldiery echoing to the skies, everything raucous with cheering, the guns and trumpets, the coins tossed to the crowd— and me, carried aloft like some sublime being, me the author and cause of all this magnificence. Well, you'd have said the Scipios, the Aemilii and the Augusti were a load of grotty old skinflints compared to me.

From *Julius Exclusus*, 1514 (Tr. AB)

Hans Christian Andersen, in his mild-mannered way, expresses his own doubts about the Catholic approach to the hearts and minds of its congregations:

A Protestant reaction to the Church of Rome

Most persons require some sensual provocative, ere on fixed days and hours they are able to raise their minds to devotion; and the Catholic Church service has such an influence, but it loses too much by the ceremonies. It seems as if the Church had not rightly understood the doctrine that, unless we be as children, we cannot enter the Kingdom of Heaven—for it often regards its congregation as children, who see and believe, who live in dreams more than in thought.

Every festival that I have seen in Rome included a really fine idea or thought; but the explication thereof was often, if I may use the expression, made too corporeal. They would show to the external sense what only belongs to feeling, and hence a soulless caricature, not a devotional picture, was presented to the view.

I believe that all well-educated Catholics will agree with me in this; for whenever my religious feelings have been wounded at these festivals, I never saw any other congregation than people of the very lowest class, whose mental conceptions stand on a level with the child's.

From *A Poet's Bazaar*, 1842, Tr. Charles Beckwith

THE VATICAN AT WAR

For much of the Middle Ages the Italian peninsula was torn by wars between the opposing powers of France and Spain. In 1527 Pope Clement VII paid dearly for his French sympathies: the troops of the Spanish emperor Charles V were sent to sack Rome, which they did with ruthlessness and brutality. Pope Clement fled for safety to Castel Sant'Angelo on the Tiber bank. Here he was protected in the massive fortress, once the mausoleum of the emperor Hadrian, which was defended by loyal troops. Among the gunners was the Florentine

goldsmith Benvenuto Cellini, who has left a vivid and
self-aggrandising account of the battle:

Benvenuto Cellini on the Sack of Rome

Upon the ramparts where we took our station several young men were lying killed by the besiegers;
the battle raged there desperately, and there was the
densest fog imaginable. I turned to Alessandro and
said: 'Let us go home as soon as we can, for there
is nothing to be done here; you see the enemies are
mounting, and our men are in flight.' Alessandro, in
a panic, cried: 'Would God that we had never come
here!' and turned in maddest haste to fly. I took him
up somewhat sharply with these words: 'Since you
have brought me here, I must perform some action
worthy of a man'; and directing my arquebus where
I saw the thickest and most serried troop of fighting
men, I aimed exactly at one whom I remarked to
be higher than the rest; the fog prevented me from
being certain whether he was on horseback or on
foot. Then I turned to Alessandro and Cecchino,
and bade them discharge their arquebuses, showing
them how to avoid being hit by the besiegers. When
we had fired two rounds apiece, I crept cautiously
up to the wall, and observing among the enemy a
most extraordinary confusion, I discovered afterwards that one of our shots had killed the Constable
of Bourbon; and from what I subsequently learned,

he was the man whom I had first noticed above the heads of the rest.

Quitting our position on the ramparts, we crossed the Campo Santo, and entered the city by St Peter's; then coming out exactly at the church of Santo Agnolo, we got with the greatest difficulty to the great gate of the castle; for the generals Renzo di Ceri and Orazio Baglioni were wounding and slaughtering everybody who abandoned the defence of the walls. By the time we had reached the great gate, part of the foemen had already entered Rome, and we had them in our rear. The castellan had ordered the portcullis to be lowered, in order to do which they cleared a little space, and this enabled us four to get inside…I ascended to the keep, and at the same instant Pope Clement came in through the corridors into the castle; he had refused to leave the palace of St Peter earlier, being unable to believe that his enemies would effect their entrance into Rome.

Having got into the castle in this way, I attached myself to certain pieces of artillery, which were under the command of a bombardier called Giuliano Fiorentino. Leaning there against the battlements, the unhappy man could see his poor house being sacked, and his wife and children outraged; fearing to strike his own folk, he dared not discharge the cannon, and flinging the burning fuse upon the ground, he wept as though his heart would break, and tore his cheeks with both his hands. Some of the other bombardiers were behaving in like manner; seeing which, I took one of the matches, and got the assistance of a few men who were not overcome by their emotions. I aimed some swivels and falconets at points where I saw it would be useful, and killed with them a good number of the enemy. Had it not been for this, the troops who poured into Rome that morning, and were marching straight upon the castle, might possibly have entered it with ease, because the artillery was doing them no damage. I went on firing under the eyes of several cardinals and lords, who kept blessing me and giving me the heartiest encouragement. In my enthusiasm I strove to achieve the impossible; let it suffice that it was I who saved the castle that morning.

From the *Autobiography*, late 1550s,
Tr. John Addington Symonds

The popes against Garibaldi in 1849

The siege of 1849, when French troops ousted Garibaldi's republican army and restored the pope to power, is evoked by the Victorian poet Arthur Hugh Clough in *Amours de Voyage*. The 'hero' of the poem-novel, the clever but feeble Claude, intellectual tourist and ineffectual lover, describes the battle from the point of view of the ordinary people, many of them tourists, all of them bewildered, uninformed and powerless:

Yes, we are fighting at last, it appears.

This morning as usual,

Murray[2], as usual, in hand, I enter the Caffè Nuovo;

Seating myself with a sense as it were of a change

in the weather,

Not understanding, however, but thinking

mostly of Murray,

And, for to-day is their day, of the Campidoglio Marbles;

Caffè-latte! I call to the waiter,—and *Non c'è latte*,

This is the answer he makes me, and this is the

sign of a battle.

So I sit: and truly they seem to think any one else more

Worthy than me of attention. I wait for my milkless *nero*,

Free to observe undistracted all sorts and sizes of persons,

Blending civilian and soldier in strangest costume,

coming in, and

Gulping in hottest haste, still standing, their coffee—

withdrawing

Eagerly, jangling a sword on the steps, or jogging a musket

Slung to the shoulder behind. They are fewer,

moreover, than usual,

Much and silenter far; and so I begin to imagine

Something is really afloat. Ere I leave, the Caffè is empty,

Empty too the streets, in all its length the Corso

Empty, and empty I see to my right and left the Condotti.

---

2 Murray's *Handbook to Rome*. The rights to the famous series were acquired in 1915 by the Muirhead brothers, founders of the Blue Guides.

Twelve o'clock, on the Pincian Hill, with lots of English,
Germans, Americans, French—the Frenchmen,
$$\hspace{10em}\text{too, are protected—}$$
So we stand in the sun, but afraid of a probable shower;
So we stand and stare, and see, to the left of St Peter's,
Smoke, from the cannon, white,—but that is at
$$\hspace{10em}\text{intervals only,—}$$
Black, from a burning house, we suppose, by the
$$\hspace{12em}\text{Cavalleggieri;}$$
And we believe we discern some lines of men descending
Down through the vineyard-slopes, and catch a
$$\hspace{12em}\text{bayonet gleaming.}$$
Every ten minutes, however—in this there is
$$\hspace{10em}\text{no misconception—}$$
Comes a great white puff from behind
$$\hspace{8em}\text{Michel Angelo's dome, and}$$
After a space the report of a real big gun—
$$\hspace{10em}\text{not the Frenchman's!—}$$
That must be doing some work. And so we watch
$$\hspace{10em}\text{and conjecture.}$$
Shortly, an Englishman comes, who says he has
$$\hspace{10em}\text{been to St Peter's,}$$
Seen the Piazza and troops, but that is all he can tell us;
So we watch and sit, and, indeed, it begins to be tiresome.
All this smoke is outside; when it has come to the inside,
It will be time, perhaps, to descend and retreat to our houses.
Half-past one, or two. The report of small arms frequent,
Sharp and savage indeed; that cannot all be for nothing:

So we watch and wonder; but guessing is tiresome, very.
Weary of wondering, watching, and guessing,

                                    and gossiping idly,
Down I go, and pass through the quiet streets

                                    with the knots of
National Guards patrolling, and flags hanging out at

                                    the windows,
English, American, Danish—and, after offering to help an
Irish family moving *en masse* to the Maison Serny,
After endeavouring idly to minister balm to the trembling
Quinquagenarian fears of two lone British spinsters,
Go to make sure of my dinner before the enemy enter.
But by this there are signs of stragglers returning; and voices
Talk, though you don't believe it, of guns

                                    and prisoners taken;
And on the walls you read the first bulletin

                                    of the morning—
This is all that I saw, and all that I know of the battle.

                        From *Amours de Voyage*, 1849

St Peter's in the Second World War

Raleigh Trevelyan, himself an Italy veteran of WWII, writes vividly of the liberation of Rome in the summer of 1944, as American troops entered the city and the Germans left it:

In the Vatican the elder Tittmann boy, Haroldino, aged fifteen, wrote in his diary: 'Today we did nothing except watch the Germans retreat. I got the best view of all, as I had gone into the nuns' garden, which overlooks the road on which the Germans were retreating…They were extensively using horses to draw carriages, waggons and every kind of contraption you could think of. Some were even on bicycles. They had stolen all Rome's horse-drawn cabs… One felt rather sorry for them; they looked so young. Some were tired and dirty…There were long columns marching…Some had to carry machine-guns on their shoulders. They looked terribly depressed. Some stopped right below me and sat on the grass. Others bought some filthy lemonade from a little stand also right below me. I must say that the Romans were very kind to them, although they were immensely relieved to see them leaving. They gave the Germans drinks and cigarettes. It is in the character of the Romans to be kind to everybody in trouble.

D'Arcy Osborne[3] watched the retreat down the 'rather slummy street' from the roof of the Santa Marta hospice, 'but it became too social up there so I came down and watched dive-bombing behind the radio masts from my room.' As Haroldino added, one could actually see the bombs dropping and little spurts of flame from the machine-guns. 'It was rather sickening to see tired German boys walking past us and

3 Francis D'Arcy Godolphin Osborne, British Ambassador to the Holy See.

then watch them being dive-bombed and strafed.'

From time to time explosions and rifle-fire could be heard. Osborne was told that the latter was due to civilians looting shops. The Germans blew up patrol and ammunition dumps at the Macao barracks and the Verano cemetery. They also succeeded in destroying the Fiat works in Viale Manzoni and three railway yards, but patriots saved many public buildings, in particular the main telephone exchange, by removing the detonators from mines. No attempt was made to blow up the main bridges.

A blond German soldier smelling of sweat and fear asked Josette Bruccoleri the way to Florence, and she gave him some cherries. 'I saw young boys of about seventeen and eighteen years old, exhausted and half-starved, hardly able to walk. Some were crying, it was pitiful, others were more courageous, perhaps older, and marched in threes, singing.' Vera Cacciatore, the curator the Keats-Shelley house, saw them going down the Corso, mostly very young and in rags, usually singing and shouting. The Italians stood back—they did not harass them, it would have been like hitting someone who was dying. Once in Piazza di Spagna some Germans fired into a crowd and a man dropped.

Mrs Cacciatore afterwards walked to Piazza del Popolo. It was deserted, except for two people, a beggar and a prostitute under the arch. 'You read about invasions, but it is extraordinary actually to be present when two armies are going through a city. We had no water, gas or electricity, only the telephone. There was a complete breakdown of services, a void, no government at all.'...

During the afternoon placards appeared everywhere in Italian: 'Come to St Peter's at six o'clock to thank the Pope.' Mother Mary St Luke was in the huge crowd that packed the Piazza. 'The afternoon light slanted across the roof of the Basilica, spilling torrents of golden light on the sea of colour below. With the flags and banners, it looked like a herbaceous border in full bloom. Soldiers in battle-dress provided an olive-drab background.' Ceremonial draping was thrown over the parapet of the central balcony and the great bell ceased to toll. Then the slender white figure of the Pontiff appeared and raised his hand for silence. He seemed to shimmer. Every phrase in his short speech over the microphone brought a crash of applause.

From that balcony one looks across the Tiber, across ochre and amber roofs, to the Quirinale palace and the Campidoglio, and to the starkly white Victor Emmanuel monument, symbol of the unification of Italy and the overthrow of Papal temporal power. On this historic day, 5 June 1944, Romans in their hundreds of thousands knelt before not only the Vicar of Christ but the personification of deliverance from the tyranny of a new Risorgimento.

From *Rome '44: The Battle for the Eternal City*

THE ART

'*Rome contains more objects of interest than perhaps any other place in the world.*' Herman Melville

'*Artists produce at Rome what they are incapable of conceiving elsewhere.*' Thomas Medwin (cousin of Shelley)

All Grand Tourists in the 18th and 19th centuries included Rome in their itinerary. As William Cowper put it in his *Progress of Error*, a young blade could be expected to describe the following trajectory:

From school to Cam or Isis, and thence home;
And thence with all convenient speed to Rome...

They came to see the art. There were those among them, of course, who treated the whole adventure as an extended stag weekend (Thomas Gray and Horace Walpole quarrelled and parted because Gray wanted to see the art and Walpole wanted to stay up late), but the more serious-minded devoted themselves to the study of painting and sculpture, and wrote reams and reams about it, in essays, letters home, diaries, novels, sometimes eloquently, sometimes badly, and with a naivety that was by turns touching and embarrassing. Some attempted to make a career out of what they had learned, either as a tour guide in Rome itself or by giving lectures back home. Herman Melville chose the latter course—though his lectures were unexpectedly dull for such a great novelist, and there are records of disappointed audiences. In her *Ariadne*, a whimsical work enormously successful when it came out in 1877, the English writer Ouida evokes the life of the artist at Rome, in prose that is both enjoyably bad and revealingly naive:

Ouida on the life of an art student in Rome

There can be hardly any life more lovely upon earth than that of a young student of art in Rome. With the morning, to rise to the sound of countless bells [and see the] shadows of the night steal away softly from off the city, releasing, one by one, dome and spire, and cupola and roof, till all the wide white wonder of the place reveals itself under the broad brightness of full day; to go down into the dark cool streets, with the pigeons fluttering in the fountains, and the sounds of the morning chants coming from many a church door and convent window, and little scholars and singing children going by with white clothes on, or scarlet robes, as though walking forth from the canvas of Botticelli or Garofalo; to eat frugally, sitting close by some shop of flowers and birds, and watching all the while the humours and the pageants of

the streets by quaint corners, rich with sculptures of
the Renaissance, and spanned by arches of architects
that builded for Agrippa, under grated windows
with arms of Frangipani or Colonna, and pillars that
Apollodorus[1] raised; to go into the great courts of
palaces, murmurous with the fall of water, and…
thence into the vast chambers where the greatest
dreams that men have ever had are written on panel
and on canvas, and the immensity and the silence of
them all are beautiful and eloquent with dead men's
legacies to the living, where the Hours and the Sea-
sons frolic beside the Maries at the Sepulchre, and
Adonis bares his lovely limbs, in nowise ashamed
because St Jerome and St Mark are there; to study
and muse, and wonder and be still, and be full of the
peace which passes all understanding, because the
earth is lovely as Adonis is, and life is yet unspent;
to come out of the sacred light, half golden, and half
dusky, and full of many blended colours, where the
marbles and the pictures live; to come out where the
oranges are all aglow in the sunshine, and the red
camellias are pushing against the hoary head of the
old stone Hermes, and to go down the width of the
mighty steps into the gay piazza, alive with bells toll-
ing, and crowds laughing…and to get away from it all

1 Apollodorus of Damascus, favourite architect of Trajan. He built Trajan's
Forum and Markets.

with a full heart, and ascend to see the sun set from the terrace of the Medici…and watch the flame-like clouds stream homewards behind St Peter's, and the pines of Monte Mario grow black against the west, till the pale green of the evening spreads itself above them, and the stars arise; and then, with a prayer— be your faith what it will—a prayer to the Unknown God, to go down again through the violet-scented air and the dreamful twilight, and so,—with unspeakable thankfulness, simply because you live, and this is Rome,—so homeward.

From *Ariadne: The Story of a Dream*, 1877

Half a century before Ouida, Edward Lear outlined his daily round. He was lodged near the Spanish Steps, in the foreign artist's quarter, on Via del Babuino. Here he describes, without a single idealised Classical reference, exactly what he did every day:

Edward Lear on his daily routine

At eight I go to the Café[2], where all the artists breakfast, and have two cups of coffee and two toasted rolls—for 6½d and then—I either see sights—make calls—draw out of doors—or, if wet—have models indoors till four. Then most of the artists walk on the Pincian Mount (a beautiful garden overlooking all

2 Caffè Greco on Via Condotti.

Rome, and from which such sunsets are seen!)—and at five we dine very capitally at a *trattoria* or eating house, immediately after which Sir W. Knighton and I walk to the Academy—whence after two hours we return home. This is my present routine but there are such multitudes of things to see in Rome that one does not get settled in a hurry, and by the bye I shall get more into the way of painting more at home, for I shall have two or three water coloured drawings ordered already, so *I shall not starve*.

Letter to his sister, 1837

Foreign artists in Rome find their way into fiction, too. Henry James in his novel *Roderick Hudson* brilliantly portrays the squandering of talent of a sculptor of genius, who finds himself unable to put his patron's generosity to good use. He suffers from artist's block, discovers that he no longer has any interest or point of junction with the plain life and the plain girl he has left behind him in small-town America, and falls helplessly in love with the unattainable Christina Light. Throwing his talent to the four winds, he embarks on a life of dissipation, even smashing a half-completed sculpture in front of the very eyes of the man who commissioned it—and who was prepared to pay five thousand dollars for the finished product—because he considers the man small-minded and the commission unworthy of a sculptor's chisel. The following extract shows him newly installed in Rome, full of hope and promise, the darling of the expatriate circle, in rooms and a studio near the Corso, close to the lodging of his friend and patron Rowland, the man who first spotted his genius and brought him to Rome, in the fond belief that the city's influence would bring his budding ability to full flower. Rowland is, meanwhile, secretly in love with Roderick's fiancée Mary. To Rowland, it seems, the young sculptor has it all:

Henry James on the agreeable life of a sculptor

Roderick went to work and spent a month shut up in his studio; he had an idea, and he was not to rest till he had embodied it. He had established himself in the basement of a huge, dusky, dilapidated house, in that long, tortuous, and pre-eminently Roman street which leads from the Corso to the bridge of St Angelo. The black archway which admitted you might have served as the portal to the Augean stables, but you emerged presently upon a mouldy little court, of which the fourth side was formed by a narrow terrace, overhanging the Tiber. Here, along the parapet, were stationed half a dozen shapeless fragments of sculpture, with a couple of meagre orange trees in terracotta tubs, and an oleander that never flowered. The unclean, historic river swept beneath; behind were dusky, reeking walls, spotted here and there with hanging rags and flower-pots in windows; opposite, at a distance, were the bare brown banks of

the stream, the huge rotunda of St Angelo, tipped
with its seraphic statue, the dome of St Peter's, and
the broad-topped pines of the Villa Doria. The place
was crumbling and shabby and melancholy, but the
river was delightful, the rent was a trifle, and everything was picturesque. Roderick was in the best humour with his quarters from the first, and was certain that the working mood there would be intenser
in an hour than in twenty years of Northampton. His
studio was a huge, empty room with a vaulted ceiling, covered with vague, dark traces of an old fresco,
which Rowland, when he spent an hour with his
friend, used to stare at vainly for some surviving co-
herence of floating draperies and clasping arms. Roderick had lodged himself economically in the same
quarter. He occupied a fifth floor on the Ripetta, but
he was only at home to sleep, for when he was not
at work he was either lounging in Rowland's more
luxurious rooms or strolling through streets and
churches and gardens...At times when [Rowland]
saw how the young sculptor's day passed in a single sustained pulsation, while his own was broken
into a dozen conscious devices for disposing of the
hours, and intermingled with sighs, half suppressed,
some of them, for conscience' sake, over what he
failed of in action and missed in possession—he felt
a pang of something akin to envy.

From *Roderick Hudson*, 1875

THE NATURE & EFFECT OF ROMAN ART

The museums of Rome have extensive collections of
Classical art. Many of the pieces were studied by artists
of the Renaissance, and were admired by young men on
the Grand Tour. The *Laocoön* and *Apollo Belvedere* in the
Vatican and the *Capitoline Venus* in the Capitoline Museums are three of the most famous examples. Macaulay
went home from a visit to the Vatican Museum 'almost
exhausted with pleasurable excitement'. Yet the ancient
art of Rome, it was generally believed by Grand Tourists, was inferior to that of Greece. In Greek sculpture
lay the genius; Roman copyists simply had talent:

Smollett on Roman art

All the precious monuments of art, which have come
down to us from antiquity, are the productions of
Greek artists. The Romans had taste enough to ad-
mire the arts of Greece, as plainly appears by the great
collections they made of their statues and pictures,
as well as by adopting their architecture and music:
but I do not remember to have read of any Roman
who made a great figure either as a painter or a statuary. It is not enough to say those professions were not
honourable in Rome because painting, sculpture and
music...were practised and taught by slaves. The arts
were always honoured and revered at Rome, even
when the professors of them happened to be slaves

by the accidents and iniquity of fortune. The business of painting and statuary was so profitable, that in a free republic, like that of Rome, they must have been greedily embraced by a great number of individuals: but, in all probability, the Roman soil produced no extraordinary genius for those arts. Like the English of this day, they made a figure in poetry, history, and ethics; but the excellence of painting, sculpture, architecture and music, they never could attain. In the Palazzo Picchini I saw three beautiful figures, the celebrated statues of Meleager, the boar, and dog[3]; together with a wolf, of excellent workmanship. The celebrated statue of Moses, by Michael Angelo, in the church of St Peter in Vincula, I beheld with pleasure; as well as that of Christ, by the same hand, in the Church of S. Maria sopra Minerva. The right foot, covered with bronze, gilt, is much kissed by the devotees. I suppose it is looked upon as a specific for the toothache; for I saw a cavalier, in years, and an old woman, successively rub their gums upon it, with the appearance of the most painful perseverance.

From *Travels through France and Italy*, 1766

Goethe was diligent in his study of the antiquities of Rome. He was captivated by a marble bust known as the *Ludovisi Juno*, a bust which he believed to be Greek,

---

3 These are now in the Vatican. The statues by Michelangelo are still *in situ*.

and therefore of great value. He had a cast of it made, which he displayed in his lodgings near the Spanish Steps (the apartment is now the Casa di Goethe museum) on his second visit to Rome:

Goethe on the influence of antique sculpture

This new apartment was spacious enough for us to display some of the plaster casts we had accumulated, nicely arranged and in a good light, which at last allowed us to enjoy these possessions. When one is constantly exposed to the sculpture of the ancients—as one is in Rome—one feels the same as when surrounded by Nature: that one is in the presence of something infinite and unfathomable. But the impression of beauty, of something exalted, however enjoyable in one way, is also unsettling. It makes one want to put one's feelings and responses into words. But in order to do that you must first fully recognise and understand what it is you are feeling. You begin to differentiate, to discriminate, to categorise, and though this isn't impossible to do, it's extremely difficult, and you find yourself back where you started, in a state of passive admiration and wonder.

But the most striking effect of all works of art is that they place you in the context in which they were made, both in time and in terms of the people involved. Surrounded by antique sculpture, you feel that Nature is in motion, you are aware of the huge diversity of human forms, and are transported back to humanity in its present form, so that the beholder is made alive and pristinely human. Even the drapery, tailored to Nature's contours and thus throwing the human body into sharper relief, is a positive element. In Rome you can enjoy this kind of backdrop every day, and it makes you covetous: you long to have such images about you, and good plaster casts, being the truest facsimiles, are the best way to achieve this. When you open your eyes in the morning, you are assailed by perfection. Your brain and all your senses are pursued by these figures and it becomes impossible to fall back into barbarism again.

The place of honour in our rooms was occupied by the *Ludovisi Juno*, valued all the more for the fact that she was so seldom and sporadically on public view, which made it seem great good fortune to be able to have her constantly before our eyes. No one of our acquaintance, when first beholding her, could pretend to be immune to that gaze[4].

From *Italian Journey*, 1786–88 (Tr. AB)

---

4 The *Ludovisi Juno* is on permanent public view today (except on Mondays) in the Palazzo Altemps, a branch of the Museo Nazionale. No one now seems awed by that gaze, that great fleshy face and thick neck, which so enslaved Goethe. She is famous, in fact, because of his love for her, not for her beauty or artistic merit. We know now that she is not Greek, nor even a Juno, but a Roman imperial propaganda piece of the 1st century AD, an image of Antonia Minor, daughter of Mark Antony, niece of Augustus and mother of Claudius.

It is interesting to compare, through the ages, which artists were admired and which were not. Hazlitt, for example, after visiting the Galleria Borghese, remarks that 'the Borghese Palace has three fine pictures, and only three—the *Diana and Actaeon* of Domenichino; the *Taking down from the Cross*, by Raphael; and Titian's *Sacred and Profane Love*'. The two artists who chiefly draw visitors to the gallery today, Bernini and Caravaggio, are not mentioned. In the age of the Grand Tour they were not considered great. It was all Raphael. And Guido Reni, a prolific artist from 17th-century Bologna who produced altarpiece art of a generally classicising turn—which seems to have turned the Victorians' heads. Hawthorne places an admiring crowd before a canvas by Reni in his *Marble Faun*; Browning, in *The Ring and the Book*, makes high claims for an altarpiece by him. Sacheverell Sitwell, writing in the 1930s, admits that tastes change. There was a time, he says, when people flocked to the Vatican to study its sculpture. But now 'our whole conception of antiquity has changed…The greater part of the sculptures of the Vatican are as dead as the sculptures of Canova and Thorvaldsen[5]. They are dead, and it is impossible to see how they can ever come to life again.'

Mark Twain, who wrote a lot about Italy, wittily takes the subject of the worship of antiquities as the theme for his short story *The Capitoline Venus*. George, an im-

5 Bertel Thorvaldsen (1770–1844) was a Danish follower of Canova.

pecunious sculptor, has been told he may not marry his sweetheart Mary until he has made fifty thousand dollars. Knowing that his new sculpture, entitled *America*, will never fetch such a sum, George turns to his childhood friend John Smitthe, who devises a cunning plan:

Mark Twain on antique versus modern

'Oh, John, friend of my boyhood, I am the unhappiest of men.'

'You're a simpleton!'

'I have nothing left to love but my poor statue of America—and see, even she has no sympathy for me in her cold marble countenance—so beautiful and so heartless!'

'You're a dummy!'

'Oh, John!'

'Oh, fudge! Didn't you say you had six months to raise the money in?'

'Don't deride my agony, John. If I had six centuries what good would it do? How could it help a poor wretch without name, capital, or friends?'

'Idiot! Coward! Baby! Six months to raise the money in—and five will do!'

'Are you insane?'

'Six months—an abundance. Leave it to me. I'll raise it.'

'What do you mean, John? How on earth can you raise such a monstrous sum for me?'

'Will you let that be my business, and not meddle? Will you leave the thing in my hands? Will you swear to submit to whatever I do? Will you pledge me to find no fault with my actions?'

'I am dizzy—bewildered—but I swear.'

John took up a hammer and deliberately smashed the nose of *America*! He made another pass and two of her fingers fell to the floor—another, and part of an ear came away—another, and a row of toes was mangled and dismembered—another, and the left leg, from the knee down, lay a fragmentary ruin!

John put on his hat and departed.

George gazed speechless upon the battered and grotesque nightmare before him for the space of thirty seconds, and then wilted to the floor and went into convulsions.

John returned presently with a carriage, got the broken-hearted artist and the broken-legged statue aboard, and drove off, whistling low and tranquilly.

He left the artist at his lodgings, and drove off and disappeared down the Via Quirinalis with the statue.

Chapter Four (Scene: The Studio)

'The six months will be up at two o'clock to-day! Oh, agony! My life is blighted. I would that I were dead. I had no supper yesterday. I have had no breakfast today. I dare not enter an eating-house. And hungry?—don't mention it! My bootmaker duns me to death—my tailor duns me—my landlord haunts me. I am miserable. I haven't seen John since that awful day. She smiles on me tenderly when we meet in the great thoroughfares, but her old flint of a father makes her look in the other direction in short order. Now who is knocking at that door? Who is come to persecute me? That malignant villain the bootmaker, I'll warrant. Come in!'

'Ah, happiness attend your highness! Heaven be propitious to your grace! I have brought my lord's new boots—ah, say nothing about the pay, there is no hurry, none in the world. Shall be proud if my noble lord will continue to honour me with his custom—ah, adieu!'

'Brought the boots himself! Don't wait his pay! Takes his leave with a bow and a scrape fit to honour majesty withal! Desires a continuance of my custom! Is the world coming to an end? Of all the—come in!'

'Pardon, *signore*, but I have brought your new suit of clothes for—'

'Come in!'

'A thousand pardons for this intrusion, your worship. But I have prepared the beautiful suite of rooms below for you—this wretched den is but ill suited to—'

'Come in!'

'I have called to say that your credit at our bank, some time since unfortunately interrupted, is entirely and most satisfactorily restored, and we shall be most happy if you will draw upon us for any—'

'COME IN!'

'My noble boy, she is yours! She'll be here in a moment! Take her—marry her—love her—be happy! God bless you both! Hip, hip, hur—'

'COME IN!!!!!'

'Oh, George, my own darling, we are saved!'

'Oh, Mary, my own darling, we are saved—but I'll swear I don't know why nor how!'

Chapter Five (Scene: A Roman Café)

One of a group of American gentlemen reads and translates from the weekly edition of 'Il Slangwhanger di Roma' as follows:

WONDERFUL DISCOVERY—Some six months ago Signor John Smitthe, an American gentleman now some years a resident of Rome, purchased for a trifle a small piece of ground in the Campagna, just beyond the tomb of the Scipio family, from the owner, a bankrupt relative of the Princess Borghese. Mr Smitthe afterward went to the Minister of the Public Records and had the piece of ground transferred to a poor American artist named George Arnold, explaining that he did it as payment and satisfaction for pecuniary damage accidentally done by him long since upon property belonging to Signor Arnold, and further observed that he would make additional satisfaction by im-

proving the ground for Signor A., at his own charge and cost. Four weeks ago...Signor Smitthe unearthed the most remarkable ancient statue that has ever been added to the opulent art treasures of Rome. It was an exquisite figure of a woman, and though sadly stained by the soil and the mould of ages, no eye can look unmoved upon its ravishing beauty. The nose, the left leg from the knee down, an ear, and also the toes of the right foot and two fingers of one of the hands were gone, but otherwise the noble figure was in a remarkable state of preservation. The government at once...appointed a commission of art-critics, antiquaries, and cardinal princes of the church to assess its value and determine the remuneration that must go to the owner of the ground in which it was found. The whole affair was kept a profound secret until last night. In the meantime the commission sat within closed doors and deliberated. Last night they decided unanimously that the statue is a Venus, and the work of some unknown but sublimely gifted artist of the third century before Christ. They consider it the most faultless work of art the world has any knowledge of.

At midnight they held a final conference, and decided that the Venus was worth the enormous sum of ten million francs!   From *The Capitoline Venus*, 1869

Incidentally, when the French painter Ingres saw the *Capitoline Venus* in 1835, on his second visit to Rome, he was indignant to find her shut away privily:

Ingres on how everything's getting worse

Pope Leo XII has done us a good turn and no mistake!
The divine *Capitoline Venus* has been closeted away,
like the women of ill repute at San Michele. You have
to get a special dispensation to see her—in fact you
need dispensations for everything. Enormous great
vine leaves now cover all the statues, male and female
alike; public places are under lock and key; everything is being touched up and St Paul's is being re-
modelled à la Valadier[6]. In fact, Rome isn't Rome any
more. The monuments are decrepit, the frescoes so
hoary it's painful to look at them, the processions and
ceremonies not as fine as they used to be. Even the
picturesque populace has disappeared. They are neither within doors nor without; everyone is dressed in
leg o'mutton sleeves. Everything is being bastardised.
But in spite of all this the faces are still beautiful, the
ancient works of art still sublime, the sky, the sun, the
structures all wonderful. And over and above all this
is Raphael, dazzling in his beauty, a truly divine being
come down to dwell among men. So all in all, Rome is
still superior to everything. Paris trails behind.

Notes et Pensées, 1835 (Tr. AB)

Art experts have often had trouble telling apart the genuine antique from the modern copy. In his autobiogra-

6 Giuseppe Valadier (1762–1839), official architect to the Papal States.

phy, the goldsmith Benvenuto Cellini has an amusing story on the subject:

Antique or modern? Cellini tells a moral tale:

There arrived in Rome a surgeon of the highest renown, who was called Maestro Giacomo da Carpi. This able man, in the course of his other practice, undertook the most desperate cases of the so-called French disease[7]. In Rome this kind of illness is very partial to the priests, and especially to the richest of them. When, therefore, Maestro Giacomo had made his talents known, he professed to work miracles in the treatment of such cases by means of certain fumigations; but he only undertook a cure after stipulating for his fees, which he reckoned not by tens, but by hundreds of crowns. He was a great connoisseur in the arts of design. Chancing to pass one day before my shop, he saw a lot of drawings which I had laid upon the counter, and among these were several designs for little vases in a capricious style, which I had sketched for my amusement. These vases were in quite a different fashion from any which had been seen up to that date. He was anxious that I should finish one or two of them for him in silver; and this I did with the fullest satisfaction, seeing they exactly suited my own fancy. The clever surgeon paid me very well,

---

7 Syphilis. His treatment involved the use of mercury.

and yet the honour which the vases brought me was worth a hundred times as much; for the best crafts-men in the goldsmith's trade declared they had never seen anything more beautiful or better executed.

No sooner had I finished them than he showed them to the Pope; and the next day following he be-took himself away from Rome. He did wisely...for not many months afterwards, all the patients he had treated grew so ill that they were a hundred times worse off than before he came. He would certainly have been murdered if he had stopped. He showed my little vases to several persons of quality; amongst others, to the most excellent Duke of Ferrara, and pretended that he had got them from a great lord in Rome by telling this nobleman that if he wanted to be cured, he must give him those two vases; and that the lord had answered that they were antique, and besought him to ask for anything else which it might be convenient for him to give, provided only he would leave him those; but, according to his own account, Maestro Giacomo made as though he would not undertake the cure, and so he got them.

I was told this by Messer Alberto Bendedio in Fer-rara, who with great ostentation showed me some earthenware copies he possessed of [the vases]. Thereupon I laughed, and as I said nothing, Messer Alberto Bendedio, who was a haughty man, flew into a rage and said: 'You are laughing at them, are you?

And I tell you that during the last thousand years there has not been born a man capable of so much as copying them.' I then, not caring to deprive them of so eminent a reputation, kept silence, and admired them with mute stupefaction. It was said to me in Rome by many great lords, some of whom were my friends, that the work of which I have been speaking was, in their opinion of marvellous excellence and genuine antiquity; whereupon, emboldened by their praises, I revealed that I had made them. As they would not believe it, and as I wished to prove that I had spoken truth, I was obliged to bring evidence and to make new drawings of the vases…By this little job I earned a fair amount of money.

From the *Autobiography*, late 1550s,
Tr. John Addington Symonds

In the later 19th century, when cultural tourism had become a craze which had spread well down into the middle classes, some writers were inclined to be snobbish about people's honest attempts to see what they thought they were supposed to see. Here is Augustus Hare, author of the famous *Walks in Rome*, cruelly patronising those less educated than himself, and probably with less leisure to spare on their continental sojourn:

Augustus Hare on how to be a good cultural tourist

There is one point which cannot be sufficiently im-

pressed on those who wish to take away more than
a surface impression of Rome: it is, never to see too
much; never try to 'do' Rome. Nothing can be more
depressing to those who really value Rome than to
see two Englishmen hunting in couples through the
Vatican galleries, one looking for the number of the
statue in the guide-book, the other finding it; than
to hear Americans describe the forum as the dustiest
heap of old ruins they had ever looked upon or say,
when asked their opinion of the Venus de' Medici[8],
that they 'guess they were not particular gone on
stone gals'; than to encounter a husband who boasts
of having seen everything in Rome in three days,
while the wife laments that, in recollection she cannot distinguish the Vatican from the Capitol, or St
Peter's from St Paul's. Better far to leave half the ruins
and nine-tenths of the churches unseen and to see
well the rest; to see them not once, but again and often again; to watch them, to learn to live with them, to
love them until they become part of life and life's recollections. And it is the same in the galleries: for what
can be carried away by those who wander over the
whole Vatican at once but a hopeless chaos of marble
limbs?—at best a nightmare in which Venus and Mercury, Jupiter and Juno, play the principal parts. But,
if the traveller will benefit by the Vatican, he must

8 This statue is in fact in Florence.

make friends with a few of the statues, and pay them
visits, and grow constantly into greater intimacy; then
the purity of their outlines and the majestic seren-
ity of their god-like grace will have power over him,
raising his spirit to a perception of beauty of which
he had no idea before, and enabling him to discern
the traces of genius in humbler works of those who
may be struggling and striving after the best, but who,
while they have found the right path which leads to
the great end, are still very far off.

From *Walks in Rome*, 13th edition, 1893

The great American art historian Bernard Berenson is
equally robust, but to us today, at least, his view seems
more realistic than Hare's. Even supposing one had
the purse of a Croesus and could afford the hefty Vatican admission fee time after time, one would need the
stamina of a Hercules for the crowds and the queues:
one cannot go 'again and often again'. In *The Passionate
Sightseer*, Berenson sums up what is still today, over half
a century later, a very real problem when trying to get
to grips with the Vatican collections: other people. Richard Holmes has a different problem: the custodians.

Richard Holmes on problems of accessibility

My own social life was very odd in Rome. Reading
Shelley's letters and poems on the sites where he
wrote them, especially in remote corners of the Fo-

rum, I perched illegally on the crumbling brickwork of the Caracalla while whole afternoons seemed to drift in absolute autumnal solitude. I was once shut in by the guards having missed their whistles, and had to climb out through a vegetable garden next door...My favourite point on the Palatine Hill, high above the Temple of Jupiter, was also temporarily out of bounds to the public, owing to subsidence, although it commanded by far the finest vista of the entire Forum. I used to arrive there during the siesta when no one was about and work undisturbed for an hour or two, until a particular guard—who got to know my routine—came and shouted at me from the far side of the wire.

From *Footsteps: Adventures of a
Romantic Biographer*, 1985

Bernard Berenson on the Sistine Chapel

In my younger years the Sistine Chapel was so accessible from the Bernini staircase to the north of St Peter's. The present arrangement is all but inhuman, and must be due to some bureaucratic convenience based on procuring the greatest inconvenience to the greatest number. Miles to walk, stairs to climb up and down, through corridors lined with artifacts that attract attention and strain your energies before you have managed to reach the Sistine Chapel. Tired out by this endless walk and annoyed by herds of tourists bellowed at by guides, I have a very poor impression of the frescoes and cannot get over it. The best Botticellis are on the outer wall where the sun prevents one seeing them. The ceiling looks dark, gloomy. The *Last Judgment* even more so. What would a dilettante, unacquainted with the subjects of these designs or their iconography, get out of them? A Hindu or a Muslim might conclude that admiration for these frescoes was part of the Christian cult and had little to do with art. How much traditional admiration still influences us; how difficult to make up our minds that these Sistine frescoes are nowadays scarcely enjoyable in the original and much more so in photographs.

From *The Passionate Sightseer*, 1960

MICHELANGELO

Berenson has a point. If you happen to visit the Sistine Chapel when it is crowded, or when a tour is in and the guide is loudly lecturing her audience, you will have a dismal time. And what *are* we meant to get out of the works of art? 'Michael Angelo,' said Hazlitt, 'is one of those names that cannot be shaken without pulling down Fame itself.' Shelley, writing less than a decade before him, seems not to have shared these qualms. Berenson's 'traditional admiration' has no influence on him:

Shelley on Michelangelo

I cannot but think the genius of this artist highly
overrated. He has not only no temperance, no modesty, no feeling for the just boundaries of art…, but
he has no sense of beauty, and to want this is to
want the sense of the creative power of mind. What
is terror without a contrast with, and a connexion
with, loveliness? How well Dante understood this
secret—Dante, with whom this artist has been so
presumptuously compared! What a thing his 'Moses'
is; how distorted from all that is natural and majestic…In the [*Last Judgement* in the Sistine Chapel],
Jesus Christ [stands] in an attitude of haranguing the
assembly. This figure, which his subject…ought to
have modelled of a calm, severe, awe-inspiring majesty, is in the attitude of commonplace resentment.
On one side of this figure are the elect; on the other,
the host of heaven; they ought to have been what
the Christians call glorified bodies, floating onward,
and radiant with that everlasting light (I speak in
the spirit of their faith) which had consumed their
mortal veil. They are in fact very ordinary people.
Below is the ideal purgatory, I imagine, in mid-air,
in the shapes of spirits, some of whom demons are
dragging down, others falling as it were by their
own weight, the others half-suspended…Every step
towards hell approximates to the region of the artist's
exclusive power. There is great imagination in many

of the situations of these unfortunate spirits. But hell and death are his real sphere. The bottom of the picture is divided by a lofty rock, in which there is a cavern whose entrance is thronged by devils, some coming in with spirits, come going out for prey. The blood-red light of the fiery abyss glows through their dark forms. On one side are the devils, in all hideous forms, struggling with the damned, who have received their sentence, and are chained in all forms of agony by knotted serpents, and writhing on the crags in every variety of torture. On the other, are the dead, coming out of their graves—horrible forms. Such is the famous 'Day of Judgment' of Michael Angelo; a kind of *Titus Andronicus* in painting, but the author surely no Shakespeare.

Letter to Peacock, 25th February 1819

These remarks might seem shocking to generations brought up to believe in Michelangelo's undisputable genius. But Shelley was by no means alone:

'O Anatomical Painter! Beware lest the too strong indication of the bones, sinews and muscles be the cause of your becoming wooden in your painting by your wish to make your nude figures display all their feeling...'

So wrote Leonardo da Vinci in his notebooks, during

a period when he was in Rome (Tr. Jean-Paul Richter, 1888). It has been convincingly suggested that these notes were inspired by what Leonardo had seen of the Sistine Chapel, decorated by an artist who was his great rival and whose Mannerist style pays little heed to anatomical exactitude.

Nathaniel Hawthorne was not completely convinced by the *Last Judgement*, either. He objects to the figure of Jesus, 'Not looking in the least like the Saviour of the world, but with uplifted arm, denouncing eternal misery on those whom He came to save. I fear I am myself among the wicked, for I found myself inevitably taking their part, and asking for at least a little pity, some few regrets, and not such a stern denunciatory spirit on the part of Him who had thought us worth dying for.' (From the *French-Italian Notebooks*).

Henry James, too, was uncertain is his response to Michelangelo. In despondent mood he escapes from what he calls the 'dingy foolery' of the Corso at Carnival time to the Capitoline Hill. But he finds it mean and its architecture uninspiring. His 'stifled hopes of sublimity' are doomed to remain stifled, and his temper is not good.

Henry James is disappointed by Michelangelo

I walked down by the back streets to the steps mounting to the Capitol—that long inclined plane, rather, broken at every two paces, which is the un-

failing disappointment, I believe, of tourists primed
for retrospective raptures. Certainly the Capitol seen
from this side isn't commanding. The hill is so low,
the ascent so narrow, Michael Angelo's architecture
in the quadrangle at the top so meagre, the whole
place somehow so much more of a mole-hill than
a mountain, that for the first ten minutes of your
standing there Roman history seems suddenly to
have sunk through a trap-door.

From Italian Hours, 1909

What pleased Henry James best on the Capitoline hill
was the gilt bronze equestrian statue of Marcus Aurelius. 'I doubt,' he writes, in *Italian Hours*, 'if any statue
of king or captain in the public places of the world has
more to commend it to the general heart. Irrecoverable
simplicity—residing so in irrecoverable Style—has no
sturdier representative. Here is an impression that the
sculptors of the last three hundred years have been la-
boriously trying to reproduce; but contrasted with this
mild old monarch their prancing horsemen suggest a
succession of riding-masters taking out young ladies'
schools. The admirably human character of the figure
survives the rusty decomposition of the bronze and
the slight "debasement" of the art; and one may call it
singular that in the capital of Christendom the portrait
most suggestive of a Christian conscience is that of a
pagan emperor.'

The same statue interested John Capgrave, too, the author of a medieval handbook to Rome entitled *Ye Solace of Pilgrimes*. The stories and descriptions in medieval pilgrims' guides are often outlandish, reflective of an atmosphere of unknowing, interpreted by rumour and hearsay, which modern minds believe—perhaps quite wrongly—that they have gone beyond. The description of the Marcus Aurelius statue is a good example. NB: In Capgrave's day the horse stood outside St John Lateran (it was moved to the Capitoline in the 16th century) and the identification with Marcus Aurelius had yet to be made:

John Capgrave tells a tall tale

Now of the horse that stands at the Lateran and of the sitter that is upon him shall be our process, for some men say that it was made in worship of great Constantine but it is not so. First will I declare unto you the shape of the image and after tell the story of what he was and why he was set there:

A great horse of brass is there, of full fair shape, which was sometime gilt, and a man eke of the same metal sitting on his back withouten saddle...This image was set there for this cause. In that time that consuls governed Rome it befell that a king came out of the East with a great strength of men and besieged Rome. In the time of consuls said I, for Rome was first governed by kings and then by two con-

suls which were chosen every year and then by emperors, of which Julius Caesar was the first. So as I
said, in that same time that counsellors governed the
city...came this king and besieged Rome. The city
was greatly afraid of this king and could not find a
means how they should avoid him. Then was there
in Rome a man of great strength. Some books say
that he was a knight, some a squire and some that he
was but of the low degree in the people, which is to
say in their language *rustico*, in ours a churl. A bold
man he was, strong and wise. Happed him to be in
the capitol where the states and their people treated
what they might do to avoid this great danger. He
stood up amongst them and said:

'What would ye give a man that should deliver you
from this distress?'

The senate answered, 'Let that man appear and ask
what he will, and he shall have it.'

'I will,' said this man, 'take this journey upon me
if that ye grant me thirty sesterces of gold and eke
make a memorial in my name, horse and man like
as I will ride. All this shall be made of brass and gilt
above on the best wise.'

The senate granted him to fulfil all his desire.

Then said he unto them, 'At midnight look ye be
ready all in ditches and caverns in the ground and in
the arches within the walls and whatsoever I bid you
do, look ye fulfil it.'

They consented to all that was said. At midnight this man leapt up on a great horse and a strong and rode forth into the field with a scythe on his back as though he would go to mow. Certain knights and squires…saw this man thus arrayed like a churl riding without a saddle and supposed not that he had been of Rome but rather some labourer of their own party and thus they cried unto him, 'Beware, churl, that thou do come not so nigh the king. Thou shall be hanged if thou touch him.'

The man heard what they said and with good deliberation he lifted up the king onto his horse, for he was a large man and a strong and the king but of little stature. Thus rode he forth crying with a loud voice, 'Rise, Romans, and defend yourselves for I have caught the king!'

The Romans caught great comfort that this king was taken. The other party lost heart that their head was absent and thus had the Romans the field, this man great worship and the peril delivered. For that same king was fain to compound with them and pay them great tribute before his deliverance was made. Then reared they this image at the Lateran with many other things than we express now, for they be wasted with age and rust as men may verily see.

From *Ye Solace of Pilgrimes*, c. 1450

CITY OF DEATH

'Rome reminds me of a man who lives by exhibiting to travellers his grandmother's corpse.' James Joyce

Joyce was not alone. For many visitors to Rome the burden of the past interfered with enjoyment of the present, seeming to weigh intolerably heavy upon the modern city, which was nowhere near as fine, as grand or as glorious as the old, and whose ruins—many as yet unexcavated, and jerry-built-upon by the constructions of the present—stuck up out of the landscape like bones from a grave, making one ever aware of the presence of death and decay, and ever reflective upon the transience and impermanence of human life. The 17th-century Spanish poet Francisco de Quevedo expresses his version of this morbid preoccupation in the following little lyric:

Quevedo on Rome as a living tomb

To Rome buried in her ruins
You look for Rome in Rome, O pilgrim!
But in Rome itself you will not find her:
What once were walls are now just bones;
The Aventine its own sepulchre.

Where the Palatine once held court all now lies waste.
And the sculpted escutcheons, eroded with age,
Reveal more of Time's vicissitudes
Than a Latin adage.

Only the Tiber remains, whose flow
Once watered a city; now grieves for a tomb,
Grieves with dolorous cadence slow.

Oh Rome, of your greatness and glory
That which was lasting has fled! What remains
Is only a frail, fleeting memory.   (Tr. AB)

John Ruskin, at the tender age of 21, was already ex-
pressing eloquently uncompromising views on things.
On Rome he was unequivocal: it is city of the dead,
where 'everyone looks like a vampyre':

Ruskin on the sepulchral horrors of Rome

There is a strange horror lying over the whole city,
which I can neither describe nor account for; it is
a shadow of death, possessing and penetrating all
things. The sunlight is lurid and ghastly, though so
intense that neither the eye nor the body can bear
it long; the shadows are cold and sepulchral; you
feel like an artist in a fever, haunted by every dream
of beauty that his imagination ever dwelt upon, but
all mixed with the fever fear. I am certain this is not

imagination, for I am not given to nonsense, and, even in illness, never remember feeling anything approaching to the horror with which some objects here can affect me. It is all like a vast churchyard, with a diseased and dying population living in the shade of its tombstones.

Letter to the Rev. T. Dale, 31st December 1840

Thomas Hardy on Rome past and present

Thomas Hardy felt the presence of death too—he was acutely sensitive to such things—but he was a much kindlier, more humane man, and he was also interested in the present, which gives his observations a poignant warmth. The following poem captures this spirit. In Rome the present seems to have little to do with the past; perhaps it is difficult to believe that the one springs from the root of the other; but nevertheless, both are to be valued:

Rome: On the Palatine

We walked where Victor Jove was shrined awhile,
And passed to Livia's rich red mural show,
Whence, thridding cave and Criptoportico,
We gained Caligula's dissolving pile.

And each ranked ruin tended to beguile
The outer sense, and shape itself as though
It wore its marble gleams, its pristine glow

Of scenic frieze and pompous peristyle.

When lo, swift hands, on strings nigh overhead,
Began to melodise a waltz by Strauss:
It stirred me as I stood, in Caesar's house,
Raised the old routs Imperial lyres had led,

And blended pulsing life with lives long done,
Till Time seemed fiction, Past and Present one.

THE ROMAN FEVER

What Ruskin calls the 'fever fear' (*see above, p. 193*) was
a very real morbid terror to most visitors. Summer fever
was a constant peril in the 18th and 19th centuries,
because the Campagna, the countryside around Rome,
was swampy and malarial. Many succumbed: one of
Nathaniel Hawthorne's daughters suffered a bout of fever so serious as to cause her father to write, 'I bitterly
detest Rome, and shall rejoice to bid it farewell forever.'
Many died: the little Protestant Cemetery is full of their
graves; Henry James makes his heroine Daisy Miller (*see
p. 91*) die of Roman fever and has her buried there. Also
buried there, in a tomb fantastically crowned by a pros-
trate angel, is the American sculptor William Wetmore
Story (the angel is his own work). He died in 1895 at
the age of seventy-six. His *Roba di Roma* is a collection

of impressions and anecdotes of the city as he knew it. He is particularly robust about the fever, and offers stern grandmotherly advice on how to stay fit and healthy and withstand the rigours of a foreign climate:

William Wetmore Story on sickness and on health

Rome has with strangers the reputation of being unhealthy; but this opinion I cannot think well founded,—to the extent, at least, of the common belief... Scarlet and typhus fevers, those fearful scourges in the North, are known at Rome only under the most mitigated forms. Cholera has shown no virulence there; and for diseases of the throat and lungs the air alone is almost curative. The great curse of the place is the intermittent fever, in which any other illness is apt to end. But this, except in its peculiar phase of *perniciosa*, though a very annoying, is by no means a dangerous disease, and has the additional advantage of a specific remedy. The Romans themselves of the better class seldom suffer from it, and I cannot but think that with a little prudence it may be easily avoided... Foreigners who visit Rome are very seldom attacked by intermittent fever; and it may truly be said, that, when they are, it is, for the most part, their own fault. There is generally the grossest inconsistency between their theories and their practice. Believing as they do that the least exposure will induce fever, they expose themselves with singular recklessness to the very causes of fever. After hurrying through the streets and getting into a violent perspiration, they plunge at once into some damp pit-like church or chill gallery, where the temperature is at least ten degrees lower than the outer air. The bald-headed, rosy John Bull, steaming with heat, doffs at once the hat which he wore in the street, and, of course, is astounded if the result prove just what it would be anywhere else,— and if he take cold and get a fever, charges it to the climate, and not to his own stupidity and recklessness. Beside this, foreigners will always insist on carrying their home habits with them wherever they go; and it is exceedingly difficult to persuade any one that he does not understand the climate better than the Italians themselves, whom he puts down as a poor set of timid ignoramuses. However, the longer one lives in Rome, the more he learns to value the Italian rules of health. There is probably no people so careful in these matters as the Italians, and especially the Romans. They understand their own climate, and they have a decided dislike of death...

What, then, are their rules of life? In the first place, in all their habits they are very regular...They are also very abstemious in their diet, and gluttony is the rarest of vices...Go to any *table d'hôte* in the season, and you will at once know all the English who are newcomers by their bottle of ale or claret or sherry or brandy; for the Englishman assimilates with difficulty, and unwillingly puts off his home habits. The fresh American will always be recognised by the morning dinner, which he calls a breakfast.

If you wish to keep your health in Italy, follow the example of the Italians. Eat a third less than you are accustomed to at home. Do not drink habitually of brandy, porter, ale, or even Marsala, but confine yourselves to the lighter wines of the country or of France. Do not walk much in the sun; 'only Englishmen and dogs' do that, as the proverb goes; and especially take heed not to expose yourself, when warm, to any sudden changes of temperature...Do not stand in draughts of cold air, and shut your windows when you go to bed...And oh, my American friends! repress your national love for hot rooms and great fires, and do not make an oven of your salon... With your great fires you will always be cold and always have colds; for the houses are not tight, and you only create great draughts thereby. You will not persuade an Italian to sit near them;—he will, on the contrary, ask your permission to take the farthest corner away from the fire. Seven winters in Rome have convinced me of the correctness of their rule. Of course, you do not believe me or them; but it would be better for you if you did,—and for me, too, when I come to visit you.

From *Roba di Roma*, 1864

THE CHURCH OF BONES

One of the most famous grisly 'sights' in Rome is the crypt of the church of the Capuchins, Santa Maria della Concezione, where the bones of long-dead friars are arranged as if they were wall-hangings. Tourists go to spook themselves with the sight, experiencing the same ghastly frisson of amusement and fear as might be felt in a Ghost Train at the circus. The whiff of *memento mori* is strong, and the church crypt has been used as the setting for more than one novel:

Helen MacInnes on the Capuchin church

The Via Vittorio Veneto is the main promenade in Rome, a wide curve of a slowly descending hill, edged with trees, sweeping down from the old Roman wall to the more commercial streets of the modern city, covering no greater distance than half of a brief mile. But it contains much. It is the street of big hotels and sidewalk cafés, of small expensive shops for perfumes and pretty shoes; of banks and imposing buildings; of lovely bareheaded girls strolling breasts out, waistlines in, between the rows of café tables; of the Capuchin church with its coarse-gowned tonsured friars welcoming visitors to view its crypts filled with dead brothers' bones—skull and ribs and pelvis laid out in patterns like a carefully arranged flower bed or a burst of fireworks. It is the street of thick trees giving dappled shade to broad sidewalks, of crowding taxis, smart cars, white-uniformed traffic policemen; of young men swerving on flatulent vespas, foreigners on foot, young Italian soldiers on wide-eyed leave in ill-fitting uniforms; of crisp, khaki-suited tourist police with a protective air; of the United States Embassy sitting placidly among walled gardens and ornamental balustrades…of neighbouring Doney's[1] where…all gather before the midday and evening meals to eye and be eyed.

From *North from Rome*, 1958

One of the most famous novels to feature the church is Nathaniel Hawthorne's *The Marble Faun*, a strange romance involving four young people, Kenyon the sculptor, Miriam the artist, Hilda the copyist and Donatello the young Tuscan count, who meet in Rome and whose mutual acquaintance involves them in a long and convoluted tale of sin and atonement, the fall from grace and banishment from Eden. It is Blake's *Songs of Innocence and Experience* in prose form, and in its day was enormously popular. Visitors to the city used to use it almost as a tourist's handbook, paying trips to the place where Hilda fed her tame doves, to the Capitoline Museums and the room of the *Resting Satyr* and *Dying Gaul* in Palazzo Nuovo, where the story begins, and to the

---

1 Caffè Doney still exists, in the Hotel Westin Excelsior.

Tarpeian Rock from where Donatello, with Miriam's tacit connivance, hurls the latter's sinister stalker to his death. The following extract is set in the Capuchin church, shortly after Donatello has killed 'Brother Antonio':

Nathaniel Hawthorne in the Capuchin church

The dead monk was clad, as when alive, in the brown woollen frock of the Capuchins, with the hood drawn over his head, but so as to leave the features and a portion of the beard uncovered. His rosary and cross hung at his side; his hands were folded over his breast; his feet (he was of a barefooted order in his lifetime, and continued so in death) protruded from beneath his habit, stiff and stark, with a more waxen look than even his face. They were tied together at the ankles with a black ribbon.

The countenance, as we have already said, was fully displayed. It had a purplish hue upon it, unlike the paleness of an ordinary corpse, but as little resembling the flush of natural life. The eyelids were but partially drawn down, and showed the eyeballs beneath; as if the deceased friar were stealing a glimpse at the bystanders, to watch whether they were duly impressed with the solemnity of his obsequies. The shaggy eyebrows gave sternness to the look.

Miriam passed between two of the lighted candles, and stood close beside the bier.

'My God!' murmured she. 'What is this?'

She grasped Donatello's hand, and, at the same instant, felt him give a convulsive shudder, which she knew to have been caused by a sudden and terrible throb of the heart. His hand, by an instantaneous change, became like ice within hers, which likewise grew so icy, that their insensible fingers might have rattled, one against the other. No wonder that their blood curdled; no wonder that their hearts leaped and paused! The dead face of the monk, gazing at them beneath its half-closed eyelids, was the same visage that had glared upon their naked souls, the past midnight, as Donatello flung him over the precipice…

And now occurred a circumstance that would seem too fantastic to be told if it had not actually happened, precisely as we set it down. As the three friends stood by the bier, they saw that a little stream of blood had begun to ooze from the dead monk's nostrils; it crept slowly towards the thicket of his beard, where, in the course of a moment or two, it hid itself.

'How strange!' ejaculated Kenyon. 'The monk died of apoplexy, I suppose, or by some sudden accident, and the blood has not yet congealed.'

'Do you consider that a sufficient explanation?' asked Miriam, with a smile from which the sculptor involuntarily turned away his eyes. 'Does it satisfy you?'

'And why not?' he inquired.

'Of course, you know the old superstition about this phenomenon of blood flowing from a dead body,' she rejoined. 'How can we tell but that the murderer of this monk (or, possibly, it may be only that privileged murderer, his physician) may have just entered the church?'

'I cannot jest about it,' said Kenyon. 'It is an ugly sight!'

'True, true, horrible to see, or dream of!' she replied, with one of those long, tremulous sighs, which so often betray a sick heart by escaping unexpectedly. 'We will not look at it any more. Come away, Donatello. Let us escape from this dismal church. The sunshine will do you good…'

From *The Marble Faun*, 1860

Another novel to make use of the Capuchin church is Hans Christian Andersen's *The Improvisatore*. The story is in many ways autobiographical, though the author transposes his childhood scenes from Denmark to Rome and introduces as the Danish character the artist Federigo, who lodges with the narrator and his mother. Here he describes one of his narrator's earliest recollections:

Hans Christian Andersen in the Capuchin church

The Capuchin monk, Fra Martino, was my mother's confessor, and she related to him what a pious child I was. I also knew several prayers very nicely by heart, although I did not understand one of them. He made very much of me, and gave me a picture of the Virgin weeping great tears, which fell, like rain-drops, down into the burning flames of hell, where the damned caught this draught of refreshment. He took me over with him into the convent, where the open colonnade, which enclosed within a square the little potato-garden, with the two cypress and orange trees, made a very deep impression upon me. Side by side, in the open passages, hung old portraits of deceased monks, and on the door of each cell were pasted pictures from the history of the martyrs, which I contemplated with the same holy emotion as afterwards the masterpieces of Raphael and Andrew del Sarto.

'Thou art really a bright youth,' said he; 'thou shalt now see the dead.'

Upon this, he opened a little door of a gallery which lay a few steps below the colonnade. We descended, and now I saw round about me skulls upon skulls, so placed one upon another that they formed walls, and therewith several chapels. In these were regular niches, in which were seated perfect skeletons of the most distinguished of the monks, enveloped in their brown cowls, their cords round their waists, and with a breviary or a withered bunch of flowers in their hands. Altars, chandeliers, and ornaments, were made of shoulder-bones and vertebrae, with bas-reliefs of human joints, horrible and tasteless as the whole idea.

I clung fast to the monk, who whispered a prayer, and then said to me,—

'Here also I shall some time sleep; wilt thou thus visit me?'

I answered not a word, but looked horrified at him, and then round about me upon the strange grisly assembly. It was foolish to take me, a child, into this place. I was singularly impressed by the whole thing, and did not feel myself again easy until I came into his little cell, where the beautiful yellow oranges almost hung in at the window, and I saw the brightly-coloured picture of the Madonna, who was borne upwards by angels into the clear sunshine, while a thousand flowers filled the grave in which she had rested[2].

This, my first visit to the convent, occupied my imagination for a long time, and stands yet with extraordinary vividness before me...

From *The Improvisatore*, 1835, Tr. Mary Howitt

THE CATACOMBS & VIA APPIA

Central to the 'death in Rome' experience are the catacombs, situated for the most part on the outskirts of

---

2 The picture described seems to be a copy of the *Madonna of Monteluce*, designed by Raphael and executed by two pupils, now in the Vatican.

the city, along the former consular roads, where the ancient Romans had also erected their funerary monuments. Many catacombs line the Via Appia. They were—and still are—on every tourist's itinerary.

Early Christians, like the Jews, inhumed their dead (the ancient Romans cremated theirs), and the locations they chose for burial were outside the city walls, underground, in labyrinthine tunnels, dug layer upon layer in the soft tufa. Bodies were mainly laid in excavated shelves in the rock, closed with stone or terracotta slabs; but there are more elaborate tomb-chambers too, and family tomb-chapels, some with primitive wall-paintings. One of the best evocations of the atmopshere of the catacombs comes from the pen of Charles Dickens:

Charles Dickens on the catacombs

Below the church of San Sebastiano, two miles beyond the gate of San Sebastiano, on the Appian Way, is the entrance to the catacombs of Rome—quarries in the old time, but afterwards the hiding-places of the Christians. These ghastly passages have been explored for twenty miles; and form a chain of labyrinths, sixty miles in circumference.

A gaunt Franciscan friar, with a wild bright eye, was our only guide, down into this profound and dreadful place. The narrow ways and openings hither and thither, coupled with the dead and heavy air, soon blotted out, in all of us, any recollection of the track by which we had come; and I could not help thinking, 'Good Heaven, if, in a sudden fit of madness, he should dash the torches out, or if he should be seized with a fit, what would become of us!' On we wandered, among martyrs' graves: passing great subterranean vaulted roads, diverging in all directions, and choked up with heaps of stones, that thieves and murderers may not take refuge there, and form a population under Rome, even worse than that which lives between it and the sun. Graves, graves, graves: Graves of men, of women, of their little children... Graves with the palm of martyrdom roughly cut into their stone boundaries, and little niches, made to hold a vessel of the martyrs' blood; Graves of some who lived down here, for years together, ministering to the rest, and preaching truth, and hope, and comfort, from the rude altars, that bear witness to their fortitude at this hour; more roomy graves, but far more terrible, where hundreds, being surprised, were hemmed in and walled up: buried before Death, and killed by slow starvation.

'The Triumphs of the Faith are not above ground in our splendid churches,' said the friar, looking round upon us, as we stopped to rest in one of the low passages, with bones and dust surrounding us on every side. 'They are here! Among the Martyrs' Graves!' He was a gentle, earnest man, and said it from his heart, but when I thought how Christian men have dealt with one another; how, perverting our most merciful religion, they have hunted down and tortured, burnt and beheaded, strangled, slaughtered, and oppressed each other, I pictured to myself an agony surpassing any that this Dust had suffered with the breath of life yet lingering in it, and how these great and constant hearts would have been shaken—how they would have quailed and drooped—if a foreknowledge of the deeds that professing Christians would commit in the Great Name for which they died, could have rent them with its own unutterable anguish, on the cruel wheel, and bitter cross, and in the fearful fire.

From *Pictures from Italy*, 1846

The Via Appia and its associations with death and burial inspired one of the finest of Peter Porter's Rome poems:

The Pines of Rome

As ghosts of old legionaries, or the upright
farmers of that unbelievable republic,
the pines entail their roots among the rubble
    of baroque and modern Rome.

Out by the catacombs they essay a contradiction,
clattering their chariot-blade branches to deny

the Christian peace, the tourist's easy frisson,
    a long transfiguration.

Look away from Agnes and the bird-blind martyrs,
the sheep of God's amnesia, the holy city
never built, to the last flag of paganism
    flying in mosaic.

Then say the pines, though we are Papal like the chill
water of the aqueducts, refreshment from a state
divinity, we know that when they tombed the martyrs
    they ambushed them with joy.

Rome is all in bad taste and we are no exception
is their motto. Small wonder that Respighi,
                'the last Roman',
adds recorded nightingales to his score *The Pines*
    of the Janiculum.

And the scent of pines as we dine at night
among the tethered goats and the Egyptian waiters
is a promise that everything stays forever foreign
    which settles down in Rome.

Therefore I nominate a Roman pine to
stand above my slab, and order a mosaic
of something small and scaly to represent
    my soul on its last journey.

From *Collected Poems*, 1999

DEATH, MURDER & EXECUTION

The last journey of the soul is the subject of a famous Latin fragment attributed to the emperor Hadrian, who died in AD 138. It consists of five short lines addressed to his own soul, which is about to make its voyage to the underworld:

Dear little wandering soul,
My body's comrade and guest,
On the brink now of descent
To a pale, stark, barren place—
There will be no more of the japes you love so much.

(Tr. AB)

Robert Browning, whose poetry is famous for its pioneering use of dramatic monologue, uses that technique to great effect in *The Ring and the Book*.

While browsing through a bric à brac stall in Florence one day, Browning had found an old booklet of papers pertaining to a murder trial, which had taken place in Rome in 1698. In the course of 21,000 lines he vividly recreates the story of Guido Franceschini, who is condemned to death for the murder of his wife Pompilia and her parents Pietro and Violante. In the extract quoted here the murdered bodies of the parents have been exposed to public view in the church of San Lorenzo in Lucina, just off the Corso. Pompilia

is not yet dead, but her wounds are so severe that her
life is despaired of:

> Just at this altar where, beneath the piece
> Of Master Guido Reni, Christ on cross,
> Second to nought observable in Rome,
> That couple lie now, murdered yestereve.
> Even the blind can see a providence here.
> From dawn till now that it is growing dusk,
> A multitude has flocked and filled the church,
> Coming and going, coming back again,
> Till to count crazed one. Rome was at the show.
> People climbed up the columns, fought for spikes
> O' the chapel-rail to perch themselves upon,
> Jumped over and so broke the wooden work
> Painted like porphyry to deceive the eye;
> Serve the priests right! The organ-loft was crammed,
> Women were fainting, no few fights ensued,
> In short, it was a show repaid your pains:
> For, though their room was scant undoubtedly,
> Yet they did manage matters, to be just,
> A little at this Lorenzo[3]. Body o' me!
> I saw a body exposed once... never mind!
> Enough that here the bodies had their due.
> No stinginess in wax, a row all round,

3 The church, in other words, San Lorenzo in Lucina, where the bodies
have been laid.

And one big taper at each head and foot.

So, people pushed their way, and took their turn,
Saw, threw their eyes up, crossed themselves,
                                        gave place
To pressure from behind, since all the world
Knew the old pair, could talk the tragedy
Over from first to last: Pompilia too,
Those who had known her—what 'twas
                                        worth to them!
Guido's acquaintance was in less request;
The Count had lounged somewhat too long in Rome,
Made himself cheap; with him were hand and glove
Barbers and blear-eyed, as the ancient sings.
Also he is alive and like to be:
Had he considerately died,—aha!
I jostled Luca Cini on his staff,
Mute in the midst, the whole man one amaze,
Staring amain and crossing brow and breast.
'How now?' asked I. ''Tis seventy years,' quoth he,
'Since I first saw, holding my father's hand,
Bodies set forth: a many have I seen,
Yet all was poor to this I live and see.
Here the world's wickedness seals up the sum:
What with Molinos' doctrine[4] and this deed,
Antichrist's surely come and doomsday near.

4 The Spanish priest Miguel de Molinos, whose doctrine, known as Quiet-
ism, was declared heretical in 1687.

May I depart in peace, I have seen my see.'
'Depart then,' I advised, 'nor block the road
For youngsters still behindhand with such sights!'
'Why no,' rejoins the venerable sire,
'I know it's horrid, hideous past belief,
Burdensome far beyond what eye can bear;
But they do promise, when Pompilia dies
I' the course o' the day,—and she can't outlive night,—
They'll bring her body also to expose
Beside the parents, one, two, three a-breast;
That were indeed a sight which, might I see,
I trust I should not last to see the like!'
Whereat I bade the senior spare his shanks,
Since doctors give her till to-night to live
And tell us how the butchery happened...

From Book II, 'Half-Rome'

While in Rome Charles Dickens witnessed the public beheading of a man convicted of robbing and then
murdering a female pilgrim. He describes it in *Pictures
from Italy*:

Dickens witnesses an execution

Suddenly, there was a noise of trumpets. 'Attention!'
was among the foot-soldiers instantly...The guillotine
became the centre of a wood of bristling bayonets and
shining sabres. The people closed round nearer, on

the flank of the soldiery. A long straggling stream of men and boys, who had accompanied the procession from the prison, came pouring into the open space… The cigar and pastry-merchants resigned all thoughts of business, for the moment, and abandoning themselves wholly to pleasure, got good situations in the crowd…After a short delay, some monks were seen approaching to the scaffold…and above their heads, coming on slowly and gloomily, the effigy of Christ upon the cross, canopied with black. This was carried round the foot of the scaffold, to the front, and turned towards the criminal, that he might see it to the last. It was hardly in its place, when he appeared on the platform, bare-footed; his hands bound; and with the collar and neck of his shirt cut away, almost to the shoulder. A young man—six-and-twenty—vigorously made, and well-shaped. Face pale; small dark moustache; and dark brown hair.

He had refused to confess, it seemed, without first having his wife brought to see him; and they had sent an escort for her, which had occasioned the delay.

He immediately kneeled down, below the knife. His neck fitting into a hole, made for the purpose, in a cross plank, was shut down, by another plank above; exactly like the pillory. Immediately below him was a leathern bag. And into it his head rolled instantly. The executioner was holding it by the hair, and walking with it round the scaffold, showing it to the people, before one quite knew that the knife had fallen heavily, and with a rattling sound.

When it had travelled round the four sides of the scaffold, it was set upon a pole in front—a little patch of black and white, for the long street to stare at, and the flies to settle on…There was a great deal of blood…Nobody cared, or was at all affected. There was no manifestation of disgust, or pity, or indignation, or sorrow. My empty pockets were tried, several times, in the crowd immediately below the scaffold, as the corpse was being put into its coffin. It was an ugly, filthy, careless, sickening spectacle; meaning nothing but butchery, beyond the momentary interest to the one wretched actor.

From *Pictures from Italy*, 1846

Edgar Allan Poe, the great American master of the horror story, includes a murder scene in Rome in his short story *William Wilson*, a tale of hidden crimes and double identities:

Edgar Allan Poe sets a murder scene in Rome

It was at Rome, during the Carnival of 18--, that I attended a masquerade in the palazzo of the Neapolitan Duke Di Broglio. I had indulged more freely than usual in the excesses of the wine-table; and now the suffocating atmosphere of the crowded rooms irritated me beyond endurance. The difficulty, too, of forcing my way through the mazes of the company contributed not a little to the ruffling of my temper; for I was anxiously seeking (let me not say with what unworthy motive) the young, the gay, the beautiful wife of the aged and doting Di Broglio. With a too unscrupulous confidence she had previously communicated to me the secret of the costume in which she would be habited, and now, having caught a glimpse of her person, I was hurrying to make my way into her presence.—At this moment I felt a light hand placed upon my shoulder, and that ever-remembered, low, damnable whisper within my ear.

In an absolute phrenzy of wrath, I turned at once upon him who had thus interrupted me, and seized him violently by the collar. He was attired, as I had expected, in a costume altogether similar to my own; wearing a Spanish cloak of blue velvet, begirt about the waist with a crimson belt sustaining a rapier. A mask of black silk entirely covered his face.

'Scoundrel!' I said, in a voice husky with rage, while every syllable I uttered seemed as new fuel to my fury, 'Scoundrel! impostor! accursed villain! You shall not—you shall not dog me unto death! Follow me, or I stab you where you stand!'—and I broke my way from the ball-room into a small ante-chamber adjoining—dragging him unresistingly with me as I went.

Upon entering, I thrust him furiously from me. He staggered against the wall, while I closed the door with an oath, and commanded him to draw. He hesitated but for an instant; then, with a slight sigh, drew in silence, and put himself upon his defence.

The contest was brief indeed. I was frantic with every species of wild excitement, and felt within my single arm the energy and power of a multitude. In a few seconds I forced him by sheer strength against the wainscoting, and thus, getting him at mercy, plunged my sword, with brute ferocity, repeatedly through and through his bosom...

From *William Wilson*, 1839

THE LAST DAYS OF KEATS

The most poignantly-described death ever died in Rome is that of John Keats. The apartment on the Spanish Steps that he rented with his friend, the struggling painter Joseph Severn, who nursed him faithfully to the end, is now the Keats-Shelley Museum and is open to the public. *The Life and Letters of John Keats*, by Lord Houghton, contains a moving account of the poet's last days. Houghton reproduces the full text of letters written by Keats himself and his friend Severn, as well as an extract from the famous elegy written by Shelley:

I have now to give the last letter of Keats in my possession; probably the last he wrote...

Rome, 30th November, 1820

My dear Brown,

'Tis the most difficult thing in the world to me to write a letter. My stomach continues so bad, that I feel it worse on opening any book,—yet I am much better than I was in Quarantine. Then I am afraid to encounter the proing and coning of any thing interesting to me in England. I have an habitual feeling of my real life having passed, and that I am leading a posthumous existence…I cannot answer anything in your letter, which followed me from Naples to Rome, because I am afraid to look it over again. I am so weak (in mind) that I cannot bear the sight of any handwriting of a friend I love so much as I do you. Yet I ride the little horse,—and, at my worst, even in Quarantine, summoned up more puns, in a sort of desperation, in one week than in any year of my life…Dr Clark is very attentive to me; he says, there is very little the matter with my lungs, but my stomach, he says, is very bad. I am well disappointed in hearing good news from George—for it runs in my head we shall all die young…Severn is very well, though he leads so dull a life with me. Remember me to all friends, and tell Haslam I should not have left London without taking leave of him, but from being so low in body and mind. Write to George as soon as you receive this, and tell him how I am, as far as you can guess;—and also a note to my sister—who walks about my imagination like a ghost—she is so like Tom⁵. I can scarcely bid you good bye, even in a letter. I always made an awkward bow.

God bless you!

John Keats

[*Keats' condition continued to deteriorate. Two months into the new year, on 15th January 1821, Severn wrote the following, as quoted by Houghton:*]

Torlonia, the banker, has refused us any more money; the bill is returned unaccepted, and to-morrow I must pay my last crown for this cursed lodging place: and what is more, if he dies, all the beds and furniture will be burnt and the walls scraped and they will come on me for a hundred pounds or more! But above all, this noble fellow lying on the bed and without the common spiritual comforts that many a rogue and fool has in his last moments! If I do break down it will be under this; but I pray that some angel of goodness may yet lead him through this dark wilderness.

If I could leave Keats for a time I could soon raise money by my painting, but he will not let me out of his sight, he will not bear the face of a stranger. I would rather cut my tongue out than tell him I

5 Keats' brother Tom had died in 1818. George, another brother, lived to the age of forty-four. His sister, Fanny, died in her eighties.

must get the money—that would kill him at a word. You see my hopes of being kept by the Royal Academy will be cut off, unless I send a picture by the spring…Dr Clark is still the same, though he knows about the bill: he is afraid the next change will be to diarrhoea. Keats sees all this—his knowledge of anatomy makes every change tenfold worse: every way he is unfortunate, yet every one offers me assistance on his account. He cannot read any letters, he has made me put them by him unopened. They tear him to pieces—he dare not look on the outside of any more: make this known.

[*Six weeks later, Keats was dead. Houghton again quotes a letter from Severn*]

Feb. 27th.—He is gone; he died with the most perfect ease—he seemed to go to sleep. On the twenty-third, about four, the approaches of death came on. 'Severn—I—lift me up—I am dying—I shall die easy—don't be frightened—be firm, and thank God it has come.' I lifted him up in my arms. The phlegm seemed boiling in his throat, and increased until eleven, when he gradually sunk into death—so quiet that I still thought he slept. I cannot say now, I am broken down by four nights' watching, no sleep since, and my poor Keats gone. Three days since, the body was opened: the lungs were completely gone. The doctors could not imagine by what means he had lived these two months. I followed his dear body to the grave on Monday, with many English. They take such care of me here—that I must else have gone into a fever. I am better now—but still quite disabled.

The Police have been. The furniture, the walls, the floor, must all be destroyed and changed, but this is well looked to by Dr Clark.

The letters I put into the coffin with my own hand. This goes by the first post.

Keats was buried in the Protestant cemetery at Rome, one of the most beautiful spots on which the eye and heart of man can rest. It is a grassy slope, amid verdurous ruins of the Honorian walls of the diminished city, and surmounted by the pyramidal tomb which Petrarch ascribed to Remus, but which antiquarian truth has ascribed to a humbler name of Caius Cestius, a Tribune of the people, only remembered by his sepulchre. In one of those mental voyages into the past which often precede death, Keats had told Severn that 'he thought the intensest pleasure he had received in life was in watching the growth of flowers': and another time, after lying a while still and peaceful, he said, 'I feel the flowers growing over me.' And there they do grow, even all the winter long— violets and daisies mingling with the fresh herbage, and, in the words of Shelley, 'making one in love with death, to think that one should be buried in so sweet a place.'

Ten weeks after the close of his holy work of friendship and charity, Mr Severn wrote to Mr Haslam:— 'Poor Keats has now his wish—his humble wish, he is at peace in the quiet grave. I walked there a few days ago, and found the daisies had grown all over it. It is one of the most lovely retired spots in Rome.'...Thus too in the *Adonaïs*[6], that most successful imitation of the spirit of the Grecian elegy, devoted to the memory of one who had restored Grecian mythology to its domain of song, this place is consecrated.

Go thou to Rome,—at once the Paradise,
   The grave, the city, and the wilderness;
   And where its wrecks like shattered mountains rise,
   And flowering weeds, and fragrant copses dress
   The bones of Desolation's nakedness;
   Pass, till the Spirit of the spot shall lead
   Thy footsteps to a slope of green access,
   Where, like an infant's smile, over the dead
A light of laughing flowers along the grass is spread;

And gray walls moulder round, on which dull Time
   Feeds, like slow fire upon a hoary brand;
   And one keen pyramid with wedge sublime,

6 By Shelley: *Adonaïs, an Elegy on the Death of John Keats.*

Pavilioning the dust of him who planned
This refuge for his memory, doth stand
Like flame transformed to marble; and beneath
A field is spread, on which a newer band
Have pitched in Heaven's smile their camp of death,
Welcoming him we lose with scarce extinguished
                                            breath…

And a few years after this was written, in the extended burying-ground, a little above the grave of Keats,
was placed another tomb-stone, recording that below
rested the passionate and world-worn heart of Shelley
himself—'Cor Cordium'.

From *The Life and Letters of John Keats*, 1867

Forty years later, Severn returned to Rome as British
Consul. When he died there, at the age of eighty-five,
he was laid to rest by his friend. The two now lie side
by side.

In 1890 the Swedish physician Axel Munthe set up
consulting rooms in the house that had been Keats's.
His *Story of San Michele* contains many amusing—
and often poignant—anecdotes about his patients in
Rome. Below is his account of a case of diphtheria in
the Grand Hotel. The Hotel (now the St Regis Grand),
near the Baths of Diocletian, was opened in 1894 by
César Ritz, four years before the famous Ritz Hotel in
Paris (and twelve years before the Ritz in London).

Axel Munthe struggles with a case of diphtheria

Late one evening I was summoned to the Grand Hotel
by an urgent message from an American gentleman
with a letter of introduction from Professor Weir-
Mitchell[7]. I was met in the hall by a furious-looking
little man who told me in great agitation that he had
just arrived by the *train de luxe* from Paris. Instead of
the best suite of rooms he had reserved, he and his
family had been crammed into two small bedrooms
with no sitting-room and not even a bath-room. The
director's wire that the hotel was full had been sent too
late and never reached him. He had just telegraphed
to Ritz to protest against this sort of treatment. To
make matters worse his little boy was ill with a fever-
ish cold, his wife had been sitting up with him the
whole night in the train, would I be kind enough to
come and see him at once? Two little children were
lying asleep in one bed, face to face, almost lips to
lips. The mother looked anxiously at me and said the
boy had been unable to swallow his milk, she feared
he had a sore throat. The little boy was breathing la-
boriously with wide-open mouth, his face was almost
blue. I put the little girl still asleep on the mother's
bed and told her the boy had diphtheria and that I
must send for a nurse at once. She said she wanted

7 Silas Weir-Mitchell (1829–1914), American neurologist and writer. Like
Munthe, he was particularly interested in the treatment of hysteria and female neurosis.

to nurse the boy herself. I spent the night scraping off the diphtheric membranes from the boy's throat, he was almost choking. Towards daybreak I sent for Doctor Erhardt to help me with the tracheotomy, the boy was on the point of suffocation. The action of the heart was already so bad that he dared not give him chloroform, we hesitated to operate, we feared the boy might die under the knife. I sent for the father; at the mention of the word diphtheria he rushed out of the room, the rest of the conversation took place through the half-opened door. He would not hear of an operation, spoke of sending for all the leading doctors of Rome to have their opinion. I said it was unnecessary and besides too late, the decision of operation or no operation remained with Erhardt and me. I wrapped a blanket round the little girl and told him to take her to his room. He said he would give a million dollars to save the life of his son. I told him it was not a question of dollars and banged the door in his face. The mother remained by the side of the bed, watching us with terror in her eyes. I told her that the operation might have to be done at any moment, it would take at least an hour to get a nurse, she would have to help us. She nodded her assent without saying a word, her face twitching under the effort to keep back her tears, she was a brave and fine woman. While I was putting a clean towel on the table under the lamp and preparing the instruments, Erhardt told me that by a strange coincidence he had received that very morning through the German Embassy a sample of Behring's new anti-diphtheric serum…It had, as I knew, already been tried with remarkable success in several German clinics. Should we try the serum? There was no time for discussion, the boy was sinking rapidly, we both thought his chances very small. With the consent of the mother we decided to inject the serum. The reaction was terrific and almost instantaneous. His whole body turned black, his temperature sprang up to a hundred and six, suddenly to drop under normal in a violent shivering fit. He was bleeding from his nose and from his bowels, the action of the heart became very irregular, symptoms of immediate collapse set in. None of us left the room during the whole day, we expected him to die at any moment. To our surprise his breathing became easier towards evening, the local conditions of the throat seemed somewhat better, the pulse less irregular. I begged old Erhardt to go home for a couple of hours' sleep, he said he was too interested in watching the case to feel any fatigue. With the arrival of Soeur Philippine, the English Blue Sister, one of the best nurses I have ever had, the rumour that diphtheria had broken out on the top floor had spread like wildfire all over the crowded hotel. The director sent me word that the boy must be removed at once to a hospital or nursing home. I answered that neither Erhardt nor I would take the responsibility, he would certainly die on the way…A moment later the Pittsburgh millionaire told me through the half-open door that he had ordered the director to clear out the whole top floor at his expense, he would rather buy the whole Grand Hotel than have his son removed at the peril of his life. Towards the evening it became evident that the mother had caught the infection. Next morning the whole wing of the top floor had been evacuated. Even the waiters and the chambermaids had fled. Only Signor Cornacchia, the undertaker, was slowly patrolling up and down the deserted corridor, top-hat in hand. Now and then the father looked in through the half-open door almost crazy with terror. The mother grew worse and worse, she was removed to the adjoining room in charge of Erhardt and another nurse, I and Sister Philippine remaining with the boy.

Towards noon he collapsed and died of paralysis of the heart.

From *The Story of San Michele*, 1929

WOMEN OF ROME

'She was pleasant to talk with, and she walked with grace. She kept the house and worked in wool. That is all. You may go.' Roman woman's tombstone, Tr. M.I. Finley

The story of Roman women—the women of ancient Rome, that is—is one of a constant battle for influence in a society that tried not to let them have it. As a means to an end some chose the route of virtue and modesty; others that of seduction and hemlock. The everyday reality was probably something in between, but we do not hear much about that. We hear of paragons (Lucretia) and vixens (Messalina), of chaste wives and mothers and of shameless nymphomaniacs. In the 2nd century BC, when Rome was still a republic, the Oppian Law was introduced. This was a sumptuary law restricting the right of women to dress finely and use luxury goods. In 195 BC Roman matrons took to the streets in protest, and the law was repealed. The ultra-conservative Cato was appalled at the rioting. The spectacle of women in the streets, talking to men who were not their husbands, outraged his ideas of what was seemly. He longed for a return to the days of his ancestors, when a husband had been within his rights to kill his wife for drinking wine, and when a respectable woman stayed within doors, breeding legitimate children and keeping her mouth shut. Here he is, fulminating like a constable of the mutaween against laxity and impropriety and calling for men to lock up their wives and daughters lest those wives and daughters gain the upper hand:

Cato the Censor in support of the Oppian Law

If, Romans, every individual among us had made it a rule to maintain the prerogative and authority of a husband with respect to his own wife, we should have less trouble with the whole sex. But now our privileges, overpowered at home by female contumacy, are, even here in the Forum, spurned and trodden under foot; and because we are unable to withstand each separately we now dread their collective body...

It was not without painful emotions of shame that I, just now, made my way into the Forum through the midst of a band of women. Had I not been restrained by the respect for the modesty and dignity of some individuals among them, rather than of the whole number, and been unwilling that they should be seen rebuked by a consul, I should not have refrained from saying to them, 'What sort of practise is this, of running out into public, besetting the streets, and addressing other women's husbands? Could not each have made the same request to her husband at home? Are your blandishments more seducing in public than in private, and with other women's husbands than with your own? Although if females would let their modesty confine them within the limits of their own rights, it did not become you, even at home, to concern yourselves about any laws that might be passed or repealed here.' Our ancestors thought it not proper that women should perform any, even private business, without a director; but that they should be ever under the control of parents, brothers, or husbands. We, it seems, suffer them, now, to interfere in the management of State affairs, and to thrust themselves into the Forum, into general assemblies, and into assemblies of election: for what are they doing at this moment in your streets and lanes?...Will you give the reins to their intractable nature, and then expect that themselves should set bounds to their licentiousness, and without your interference? This is the smallest of the injunctions laid on them by usage or the laws, all which women bear with impatience: they long for either liberty—nay, to speak the truth, not for liberty, but for unbounded freedom in every particular; for what will they not attempt if they now come off victorious? Recollect all the institutions respecting the sex, by which our forefathers restrained their profligacy and subjected them to their husbands; and yet, even with the help of all these restrictions, they can scarcely be kept within bounds. If, then, you suffer them to throw these off one by one, to tear them all asunder, and, at last, to be set on an equal footing with yourselves, can you imagine that they will be any longer tolerable? Suffer them once to arrive at an equality with you, and they will from that moment become your superiors.

Translation from *The World's Famous Orations*

THE CULT OF VIRTUOUS WOMEN

The emperor Augustus (ruled 27 BC–AD 14) was well aware that for Rome to succeed as an imperial force, it needed manpower. In a drive to improve public morals and encourage Roman citizens to marry and produce legitimate offspring, he introduced a series of laws which offered incentives to married couples to have children (those who produced three sons were particularly rewarded), penalised the unmarried (by disallowing their inheritances) and discouraged adultery (by exiling offenders). Augustus was forced to obey his own strictures and banish his licentious daughter Julia to a tiny island. The rules were not always successful. In part this was because they were aimed mainly at the patrician classes and forbade marriage across the social strata. A man from the senator class, for example, who fell in love with an actress, a prostitute or a freedwoman, was not permitted to marry her—and thus many men kept the women they loved as concubines.

The kind of virtuous Roman matron that was publicly admired is portrayed by Propertius in his Elegy for the death of Cornelia. Cornelia was born into the family of the Scipios, prominent in Roman politics during the Republic and held up as role models to most Romans, who took from them their sense of moral identity and virtue. The tomb of the Scipios, close to the beginning of the Via Appia, can still be visited today, and inscriptions from it are held in the Vatican Museums. Cornelia's father was a direct descendant of the Scipio Africanus who had defeated Hannibal. Her mother, Scribonia, also from a respected family, was compelled to divorce Cornelia's father for political reasons and to marry the future Augustus. The marriage was unhappy and ended in divorce, and their daughter Julia was later exiled (*see above*). Cornelia's brother, named Cornelius Scipio like his father, embarked on a successful political career. He was nominated tribune for the second time in 16 BC, the year of his sister's death. He later fell from grace and was exiled, rumour had it because of an affair with his half-sister Julia. Cornelia died at the age of thirty (not unusual for the time). In his Elegy, Propertius makes her remind the world of her illustrious ancestry, of her unsullied character as wife and mother, and commend her children to their father's care, adjuring her husband not to mourn her death too publicly and nobly telling her children to accept a stepmother unresistingly should their father marry again:

Propertius' elegy on a Roman wife

Elegy for the tomb of a noble Roman Lady, Cornelia, daughter of Cornelius Scipio and wife to L. Aemilius Paullus

Cease, Paullus, to beset my tomb with your tears; the black door is not thrown open to any prayers: when once a death has entered the infernal jurisdiction, the ways are fast with inexorable adamant...Vows move the gods above: once the Ferryman has taken his pence, the lurid gate shuts bolt and bar on the half-consumed faggot. Such was the law the mourning trumpets proclaimed when the unkind torch was put to the fuel and made away with my person from off the bier. Marriage with a Paullus, chariots of my grandsires—what have they profited me? Or the many warrants of my good name? Cornelia has not found the Fates any less cruel: and I am a pinch of dust for five fingers to gather...

If one has honour of a grandsire's trophies, then the kingdoms of Africa tell of my grandsire the conqueror of Numantia: a second host presents the Libones on my mother's side, to challenge comparison, and either house has proud records to stand upon. In due time when maidenly frock gave place before nuptial torch, and a new kind of knot gathered up the well-beloved bride's hair, I was united to that couch of yours, Paullus, from which I must thus depart. It shall be read of me on this stone that I was the wife of one husband. I summon the ashes of my forefathers (Rome holds their memory in awe) under whose proud records Africa lies battered; I summon thee, Perseus[1], whose heart was spurred to adventure by thine ancestor Achilles, and him who shattered thy house despite Achilles thine ancestor to bear witness that I abated not the rigour of the censorial canon, and that my home had no stain to blush for...

You, my Lepidus, and you, my Paullus [her sons], are my consolation after death: my eyes were closed in your embraces. I saw my brother also twice hold his chair of office: he had been appointed consul when his sister was carried off betimes.

Daughter, born to be the pattern of your father's censorial rule, see that you copy me and hold fast by one husband. And you all must support the breed by your line: I put out from shore in my bark with a cheerful heart to think there are so many of my people to enlarge my destinies.

This is the utmost wages of womanly triumph, when frank report praises the well-deserving dead in her funeral fires.

Now I commit the children to you, the gages of our union...And if you shall grieve at all, let it be

---

1 Perseus of Macedon, defeated by Cornelia's husband's ancestor in 148 BC at the Battle of Pydna.

where they cannot witness it; when they come, make pretence to kiss them with dry eyes. Let the nights be enough time, Paullus, for you to weary out for my sake, the nights and the dreams which often by faith take on my features…

If, though, the door must see a change in the wedding-bed over against it, and a wary stepmother sit on my couch, then, my sons, do you commend and accept your father's marriage…And do not praise your mother too much: if the new is compared with her predecessor, she will turn the frankness of your talk into slights upon herself…

And so all's well: as a mother I never put on mourning; the whole flock came to attend on my funeral.

This is the sum of my pleading.

Elegies, Book IV, Tr. J.S. Phillimore

Augustus' laws inevitably appeared prudish to many, and were easy targets for ridicule. Ovid sends them up in his *Ars Amatoria* (*The Art of Love*), written at the end of the 1st century BC. This scurrilous manual on how to succeed in getting your girl (or boy) was a deliberate dig at Augustus' moral reform package—and Augustus was swift to react. Ovid was exiled from his beloved Rome to the shores of the Black Sea. In his lamentations after the event, he claims that he was exiled for a *'carmen et error'*—a song and a mistake. We think we know what the song was. The mistake remains a mystery.

Ovid on the wide choice of women in Rome

While you're still free and no one's got you on the leash, pick the girl to whom you could say 'You're the only one for me'. She won't be wafted in on the wind; you're going to have to seek her out. The hunter knows exactly where to net a stag; he knows just where the wild boars lurk. The fowler knows where to scatter his lime; the fisherman knows which waters yield most fish. So you, who are looking for the makings of a lasting love, must learn the places that girls frequent. I'm not going to suggest that you set sail on an ocean voyage or wear out your shoe-leather on a long and dusty road. Perseus brought Andromeda back from darkest India; Paris went all the way to Greece for his Helen. But Rome has so many beauties to offer, you'll soon be telling yourself that this place has it all. Beautiful girls here are as numerous as ears of corn in Gargara, grapes in Methymna, fish in the sea, birds in the trees, stars in the sky. Venus has set up shop in the city of Aeneas, her son. If you like them young, before they're quite grown up, hey presto, a veritable child will appear before you. If it's youth you want, there are thousands of girls out there—you'll be spoilt for choice. If you prefer a little age and experience, believe me, there's a whole army of them...

From *Ars Amatoria*, Book I (Tr. AB)

Robert Graves, in his novel *I, Claudius*, imagines a scene

in the Forum where Augustus harangues the men of
Rome for not producing enough legitimate children.
Claudius is the narrator, and, he argues, it is the women
who are reluctant to have children, not the men:

Robert Graves on Augustus' marriage laws

On one occasion when the Noble Order of Knights,
from whom the senators were chosen, complained of
the severity of his laws against bachelors, [Augustus]
summoned the entire order into the Market Place
for a lecture. When he had them assembled there he
divided them up into two groups, the married and
the unmarried. The unmarried were a very much
larger group than the married and he addressed
separate speeches to each group. He worked himself
up into a great passion with the unmarried, calling
them beasts and brigands and, by a queer figure of
speech, murderers of their posterity. By this time Augustus was an old man with all the petulance and
crankiness of an old man who has been at the head
of affairs all his life. He asked them, had they an hal-
lucination that they were Vestal Virgins? At least a
Vestal Virgin slept alone, which was more than they
did. Would they, pray, explain why instead of sharing their beds with decent women of their own class
and begetting healthy children on them, they squan-
dered all their virile energy on greasy slave-girls and
nasty Asiatic-Greek prostitutes?...If he had his way,

a man who shirked his social obligations and at the same time lived a life of sexual debauch should be subject to the same dreadful penalties as a Vestal who forgot her vows—to be buried alive.

As for us married men…he gave us a most splendid eulogy, spreading out his arms as if to embrace us. 'There are only a very few of you, in comparison with the huge population of the City. You are far less numerous than your fellows over there, who are unwilling to perform any of their natural social duties. Yet for this very reason I praise you the more, and am doubly grateful to you for having shown yourselves obedient to my wishes and for having done your best to man the State. It is by lives so lived that the Romans of the future will become a great nation.'…

I wanted to laugh…What was the use of Augustus addressing us in this way, when he was perfectly well aware that it was not the men who were shirking, as he called it, but the women?…I remember once hearing two of my mother's freedwomen discussing modern marriage from the point of view of a woman of family. What did she gain by it? they asked. Morals were so loose now that nobody took marriage seriously any longer. Granted, a few old-fashioned men respected it sufficiently to have a prejudice against children being fathered on them by their friends or household servants, and a few old-fashioned women respected their husbands' feelings sufficiently to be very careful not to become pregnant to any but them. But as a rule any good-looking woman nowadays could have any man to sleep with whom she chose. If she did marry and then tired of her husband, as usually happened, and wanted someone else to amuse herself with, there might easily be her husband's pride or jealousy to contend with. Nor in general was she better off financially after marriage. Her dowry passed into the hands of her husband, or her father-in-law as master of the household, if he happened to be alive; and a husband, or father-in-law, was usually a more difficult person to manage than a father, or elder brother, whose foibles she had long come to understand. Being married just meant vexatious household responsibilities. As for children, who wanted them? They interfered with the lady's health and amusement for several months before birth and, though she had a foster-mother for them immediately afterwards, it took time to recover from the wretched business of childbirth, and it often happened that her figure was ruined after having more than a couple. Look how the beautiful Julia had changed by obediently gratifying Augustus's desire for descendants. And a lady's husband, if she was fond of him, could not be expected to keep off other women throughout the time of her pregnancy, and anyway he paid very little attention to the child when it was born. And then, as if all this were not enough, foster-mothers were shockingly careless nowadays and the child often died. What a blessing it was that those Greek doctors were so clever, if the thing had not gone too far—they could rid any lady of an unwanted child in two or three days, and nobody be any the worse or wiser...

From *I, Claudius*, 1934

SEX, LOVE & CELIBACY

'I never was attached,' Shelley boasts, in his poem *Epipsychidion*, 'to that great sect,

Whose doctrine is, that each one should select
Out of the crowd a mistress or a friend,
And all the rest, though fair and wise, commend
To cold oblivion, though it is in the code
Of modern morals....'

Shelley was not faithful to either of his wives. He writes frankly about Roman women, in a way that suggests he was sizing them up:

Shelley on Roman women

The Romans please me much, especially the women, who, though totally devoid of every kind of information, or culture of the imagination, or affections, or understanding—and, in this respect, a kind of gentle savages—yet contrive to be interesting. Their extreme innocence and naïveté, the freedom and gentleness of their manners; the total absence of affectation, makes an intercourse with them very like an intercourse with uncorrupted children, whom they resemble in loveliness as well as simplicity. I have seen two women in society here of the highest beauty; their brows and lips, and the moulding of the face modelled with sculptural exactness, and the dark luxuriance of their hair floating over their fine complexions; and the lips—you must hear the commonplaces which escape from them, before they cease to be dangerous. The only inferior part are the eyes, which though good and gentle, want the mazy depth of colour behind colour, with which the intellectual women of England and Germany entangle the heart in soul-inwoven labyrinths.

Letter to Peacock, 6th April, 1819

Boswell on his amorous adventures in Rome

I must admit that in the midst of my Roman studies I indulged in sensual relaxations. I sallied forth of an evening like an imperious lion, and I had a little French painter, a young academician, always vain, always alert, always gay, who served as my jackal. I remembered the rakish deeds of Horace and other amorous Roman poets, and I thought that one might as well allow one's self a little indulgence in a city where there are prostitutes licensed by the Cardi-

nal Vicar. Thus does an ill-regulated mind assemble
scattered ideas and compose from them a principle
for action. I was, however, brought to a halt by an
unpleasant occurrence which all libertines have to
reckon with. When we walked in your room, disputing about the commerce of the sexes, you said to me
with a smile, 'Watch out for Italian girls—for several
reasons.' I discovered at Rome that your advice was
very sound.   *Letter to Rousseau*, 1765

The ancient Roman civilisation, like any other, was
much more complex and subtle than it might appear.
One does not necessarily see what one thinks one sees,
from the fragments which have survived. Is this the real
Horace speaking, for instance, the son of a freedman?
Or is he adopting a persona?

Horace on instant gratification

When you're dying of thirst do you demand to drink
from a golden cup? When weak with hunger do
you turn your nose up at anything but peacock and
turbot? When you're groin's tumescent and there's a
slave-girl or boy to hand, whom you could have right
away, would you rather burst with lust? Not me, I'm
for instant gratification. I like sex that is easy to get.
                         Satires, Book I, 2 (Tr. AB)

One would think, from all this, that true love and affection between the sexes was unknown in ancient Rome. Of course that was not the case. Catullus addresses poetry of great passion to his Lesbia. But true love makes dull reading after a while. Catullus and Lesbia do not stay together forever, and when the final break comes, the poet asks some friends to pass on a message to her: 'Repeat to my girl a few words…May she live and flourish with her fornicators, and may she hold three hundred at once in her embrace, loving not one in truth, but bursting again and again the guts of all: nor may she look back upon my love as before, which by her lapse has fallen, just as a flower on the meadow's edge, after the touch of the passing plough.' (Tr. Leonard Smithers).

The elegiac poet Propertius dedicates a number of love lyrics to the woman he calls Cynthia; but theirs was a stormy relationship. He oscillates between joy and rage. His joy when she chooses not to go on a journey to Illyria is touching: 'My Cynthia has renounced going on her new voyage. "Dear," she calls me, and Rome "very dear for my sake," and "a kingdom has no sweets without me." Narrow may be the bed, but she has chosen to sleep with me…' But when the final break comes, hell hath no fury like a poet scorned:

> I was made a mock of: the tables were laid and there
> was a gay supper party, and anybody was allowed
> to be clever at my expense.

Five years did I manage to serve you loyally: you shall often bite your nails and regret my faithfulness. I am no whit touched by tears: these were the same tricks which ensnared me; you always used to weep from deceit, Cynthia.

I shall weep at departing, but my wrongs are stronger than weeping. It is you who will not let a well enough sorted pair run in harness together.

Now farewell to the threshold which has shed tears at my pleadings, and to the door which my hand never broke despite my anger.

But as for you, let the burden of age press heavy on you with the weight of dissembled years, and come the wrinkle which bodes disaster to your good looks! Ah, when the mirror upbraids you with your wrinkles, then may you long to pull out the white hairs by the root!

May it be your turn to be denied the door and suffer the slights of pride; and may you repine when you are an old woman, and done by as you did!

These are the curses of destiny given to my page to preach: learn to dread their fulfilment for your beauty!

Elegies, Book III,
Tr. J.S. Phillimore

And yet, even after the final separation has come, even after Cynthia is dead, she haunts him still:

> Spirits do exist; death is not the end...I dreamed I saw Cynthia bending over my bed, Cynthia, just buried beside the roaring road...Her hair was the same, her eyes...She spoke to me... (Tr. AB)

In primitive societies there is often a preoccupation with female sexual activity. Fertility is all important, and men want to be sure of their line. In order to be respected, a woman must either be a wife, a mother, or celibate. The Vestal Virgins of ancient Rome were the most reverend women in the Empire. There were six of them, and they served a term of thirty years from the age of about ten. On their return to the world they were free to marry, but many preferred to remain in the Atrium, the House of the Vestals in the Forum, behind the circular Temple of Vesta, which housed the sacred fire which it was the Virgins' duty to tend: if it went out, it was believed that the State of Rome was imperilled. A Vestal who broke her vow of chastity was sentenced to be buried alive.

The novelist Elizabeth Bowen was fascinated by the Vestal Virgins, and dedicates a substantial part of her *A Time in Rome* to speculations on their lives:

Elizabeth Bowen on the advantages of celibacy

The existences of the Vestal Virgins were, as I see

it, enviable. For what they forwent as women, they were compensated in the ways women most truly enjoy. An aura surrounded them. Limelit appearances, during which everything that they said and did was above criticism, alternated with restful privacy. Their transit through streets or across the Forum left behind it a wake of awe, not untouched by sentiment, in the most profane. They were on idyllic terms with Emperors with whom it would otherwise have been impossible to be platonic. So far as the great could relish intelligence, the six had an opportunity to show it. The elevated seclusion in which they lived must have been favourable to the growth of character, as is conditioned air to the nursling plant. Vestals' counsels were harkened to; they could exercise influence, and did so. They could secure pardons: a Vestal meeting in the street a criminal being taken to execution could have him spared. Sheathed from grossnesses, insulated from dramas, scandals, the six during their sallies into the *beau monde* were free to observe these at close quarters: much must they have had to discuss, with a cool wonder, upon their return to the cool Atrium. Yet they knew, one may hope, something more than serene complacency; rendered to religion by dedication, they cannot but have been spiritualised by their unearthly duties. Moreover, what they saw of the flesh must have beautified for them their vow of chastity...

The premises known as the Atrium of the Vestal Virgins were, we recall, more than once rebuilt, lavishly, by well-meaning Emperors. Each time this must have raised dust, disorganised routine, and brought in workmen. A more trying because more regular nuisance would have been night-time disturbance by the Palatine set—the Vestals must have been constantly shocked awake. The Atrium, remember, backed on the Palatine, which rose steeply above it like a wall, and the Vestals, again remember, slept at the back. Soon after the Forum's roar had subsided, activity would begin on the built-up hillside. That now spectral honeycomb, stairs, ramps, passages, through which, moreover, zigzagged a vaulted roadway, overhung the Atrium's bedchambers—and it was by one or another of those routes that after-dinner Palatine parties, on noisy vice bent, plunged their way down into the sink of unlit Rome, and ultimately made their debauched return. The din, the echoes they kicked up must have been hideous. The Imperial ladies and their entourages went to all lengths to flaunt their errors: consequently their names have remained so bad that there seems no point in blackening them further...Where would our vocabulary be without Messalina? Yet was not this Empress, now a prototype, but an extreme example of her kind?—who, adding to nymphomania an addiction to dabbling in power politics, in almost all cases met wretched ends[2]. What mattered was, that they cost more than they were worth: they damaged the existing regard for women. The Roman matron—wise and temperate consort, guardian of everything in the *domus* that was benevolent and tender, raiser of memorable sons— came to be a receding and dimming image. Nor, for a time, did anything more individualised, original, or spirited replace her. The one career open to women outside the *domus* appeared to be a career round town; every caterwaul or titter heard in the night went to confirm masculine pessimism. Rome seems to have raised no 'new woman' till the emergence of the feminine Christian martyrs, whose independence of character, equanimity, poise, firmness, and power to discountenance should be noted, not as distinct from their saintliness but as part of it. These were the emancipates, under God.

From *A Time in Rome*, 1959

2 Messalina was the third and penultimate wife of the emperor Claudius. According to some historians, she was sexually irrepressible, and after dark would hurry from her palace on the Palatine to the Subura, a seedy district of the city, where she sold her services in a brothel. She was executed after the discovery of a plot to murder her husband.

WATER

'Rome and Carcassonne have the lovely sound of water in their streets and squares. We lived in a pension in Piazza Barberini, and I still think of the splash of the Barberini fountain in the night as part of the Roman magic.'

Freya Stark

'With such an array of indispensable structures carrying so many waters, compare, if you will, the idle Pyramids or the useless, though famous, works of the Greeks!'

Sextus Julius Frontinus, Curator of Aqueducts, 1st century AD, Tr. Charles E. Bennett

'I can think of no other European city,' says Joan Marble in her *Notes from a Roman Terrace*, 'where fountains, big and small, bring such a constant supply of water to the thirsty citizens.' She is probably right that there is no other. The ancient aqueducts of Rome, built between the 4th century BC and the 3rd century AD, supplied, during the heyday of the Empire, a staggering thousand litres a day for every head of population, an amount never surpassed since. In the 6th century AD the invading Goths cut the aqueducts and the countryside around Rome became swampy and malarial. The popes of the Renaissance made great efforts to improve the water supply, repairing old aqueducts and even building a new one. In the city itself great fountains were erected, still famous today, and some of them—the Trevi, the Fountain of the Four Rivers in Piazza Navona—are major tourist destinations in their own right. Few writers on Rome have failed to notice and comment on her abundance of running water.

Smollett on water in Rome

Nothing can be more agreeable to the eyes of a stranger, especially in the heats of summer, than the great number of public fountains that appear in every part of Rome, embellished with all the ornaments of sculpture, and pouring forth prodigious quantities of cool, delicious water, brought in aqueducts from different lakes, rivers, and sources, at a considerable distance from the city. These works are the remains of the munificence and industry of the ancient Romans, who were extremely delicate in the article of water: but, however, great applause is also due to those beneficent popes who have been at the expense of restoring and repairing those noble channels of health, pleasure, and convenience.

From *Travels through France and Italy*, 1766

Shelley on the fountains of Rome

The fountains of Rome are, in themselves, magnificent combinations of art, such as alone it were worth coming to see. That in the Piazza Navona, a large square, is composed of enormous fragments of rock, piled on each other, and penetrated, as by caverns. This mass supports an Egyptian obelisk of immense height. On the four corners of the rock recline, in different attitudes, colossal figures representing the four divisions of the globe. The water bursts from the crevices beneath them. They are sculptured with great spirit; one impatiently tearing a veil from his eyes; another with his hands stretched upwards. The Fontana di Trevi is the most celebrated, and is rather a waterfall than a fountain; gushing out from masses of rock, with a gigantic figure of Neptune; and below are two river gods, checking two winged horses, struggling up from among the rocks and waters. The whole is not ill-conceived nor executed; but you know not how delicate the imagination becomes by dieting with antiquity day after day.

Letter to Peacock, 23rd March 1819

The courtyards of many Roman *palazzi* still preserve their fountains. Mario Praz describes his delight in discovering them. Nathaniel Hawthorne describes one too, but less romantically:

Mario Praz on a courtyard fountain

It was on my own that I discovered Via Giulia, like any

other foreign tourist with a Baedeker. And the street[1] made a deep impression upon me, for it was quiet like some noble street in a provincial town; quiet like a corridor between rooms which were the courtyards of palaces, or like the nave of a church with chapels on either hand: and when one went into these courtyards one was filled with astonished reverence on account of their secret silence broken only by the gentle sound of a fountain. Of all these courtyards that of the Palazzo Ricci remained impressed upon my memory. One entered it through a great vaulted corridor opening at its far end into a gravelled space with the sky overhead between walls tapestried with ivy, and with a white statue of a woman dated 1840, holding on her knees an open book with a portrait of Dante and gazing in front of her with an air of absorption. In this place the fountain gurgled more softly than elsewhere, and from this courtyard I tore myself away unwillingly, promising myself that I would visit it often.

From *The House of Life*, 1958,
Tr. Angus Davidson, 1964

Nathaniel Hawthorne on a courtyard fountain

The courtyard and staircase of a palace built three hundred years ago are a peculiar feature of modern

---

1 Named after Pope Julius II, who laid it out, Via Giulia is a long straight street leading behind Palazzo Farnese, lined with churches and palaces.

Rome, and interest the stranger more than many things of which he has heard loftier descriptions. You pass through the grand breadth and height of a squalid entrance way, and perhaps see a range of dusky pillars, forming a sort of cloister round the court, and in the intervals, from pillar to pillar, are strewn fragments of antique statues, headless and legless torsos, and busts that have invariably lost—what it might be well if living men could lay aside in that unfragrant atmosphere—the nose. Bas-reliefs, the spoil of some far older palace, are set in the surrounding walls, every stone of which has been ravished from the Coliseum, or any other imperial ruin which earlier barbarism had not already levelled with the earth. Between two of the pillars, moreover, stands an old sarcophagus without its lid, and with all its more prominently projecting sculptures broken off; perhaps it once held famous dust, and the bony framework of some historic man, although now only a receptacle for the rubbish of the courtyard, and a half-worn broom.

In the centre of the court, under the blue Italian sky, and with the hundred windows of the vast palace gazing down upon it, from four sides, appears a fountain. It brims over from one stone basin to another, or gushes from a Naiad's urn, or spurts its many little jets from the mouths of nameless monsters, which were merely grotesque and artificial when Bernini, or whoever was their unnatural father, first produced them; but now the patches of moss, the tufts of grass, the trailing maiden-hair, and all sorts of verdant weeds that thrive in the cracks and crevices of moist marble, tell us that Nature takes the fountain back into her great heart, and cherishes it as kindly as if it were a woodland spring. And, hark, the pleasant murmur, the gurgle, the plash! You might hear just those tinkling sounds from any tiny waterfall in the forest though here they gain a delicious pathos from the stately echoes that reverberate their natural language. So the fountain is not altogether glad, after all its three centuries at play!

From *The Marble Faun*, 1860

THE ROMAN BATHS

With all the abundance of water at their disposal, it is not surprising that the ancient Romans were famed for their bath houses. The earliest of these were just that: places where one could go to wash. In later centuries wealthy citizens began to add bathing complexes to their town houses and villas, and the public baths, such as those built by the emperors Caracalla and Diocletian (3rd and 4th centuries AD), were lavish establishments, encrusted in marble and adorned with statuary, where one would go to take exercise, bathe, be massaged and perfumed, and to stroll in the gardens, meet friends and associates, even retreat to the library for a little study. The ruins of the Baths of Caracalla are especially impressive: Shelley famously wrote *Prometheus Unbound* among their fallen brickwork.

Stoical Romans sick of imperial luxury longed for a return to the fabled simplicity of their forefathers. Seneca was one of these. Just as he deplored elaborate festivals (*see p. 71*), so also he disapproved of luxuriously-appointed baths. 'We think ourselves miserable paupers unless our walls shimmer with costly cladding; unless our Alexandrian marble is set off by Numidian mosaic,' he complained (*Epistles* 86; Tr. AB). And since his lodging was above a bath house, he also suffered from the cacophonous noise. Smollett gives a detailed description of the ancient baths and how they were used. George Gissing and Henryk Sienkiewicz both found them a good setting for scenes in their historical novels.

Seneca complains of bath-house noise

I'm surrounded by noise. I live directly above a bath house. So imagine the racket—din of all kinds—which makes me hate the fact that I have ears. When the fitness addict is doing weights, when he's hard at it—or pretending to be—I hear great grunts, and when he breathes out again I hear his high-pitched puffing and blowing. Or take the lazy one, who doesn't exert himself beyond a cheap massage—

I still hear the hands slapping on his shoulders, a sound which changes depending on whether the hand is applied flat or cupped. And if a ball player should happen along, shouting out the score, that's really the bitter end. Add to all this the arrest of a rowdy or a thief, and then the noise of the man who loves the sound of his own voice, and the irrepressibles who dive-bomb into the water with an almighty splash. And apart from those whose voices, if nothing else about them, are good, there's the depilator to contend with, touting his services in his strident tones and only falling silent when tugging hairs from his client's armpit—which makes the client yelp instead. Then there are the shouts of the drinks vendor and the sausage seller, the pieman and the whole tribe of snack merchants hawking their wares, each with his own distinctive cry...

From *Moral Epistles* Book VI, 61 (Tr. AB)

Smollett on the baths of ancient Rome

Bathing was certainly necessary to health and cleanliness in a hot country like Italy, especially before the use of linen was known: but these purposes would have been much better answered by plunging into the Tiber than by using the warm bath in the thermae, which became altogether a point of luxury borrowed from the effeminate Asiatics, and tended to debilitate the fibres already too much relaxed by the heat of the climate. True it is, they had baths of cool water for the summer: but in general they used it milk-warm, and often perfumed: they likewise indulged in vapour-baths, in order to enjoy a pleasing relaxation, which they likewise improved with odoriferous ointments.

The thermae consisted of a great variety of parts and conveniences; the *natationes*, or swimming places; the *portici*, where people amused themselves in walking, conversing, and disputing together, as Cicero says, 'In porticibus deambulantes disputabant'; the *basilicae*, where the bathers assembled, before they entered, and after they came out of the bath; the *atria*, or ample courts, adorned with noble colonnades of Numidian marble and oriental granite; the *ephibia*, where the young men inured themselves to wrestling and other exercises; the *frigidaria*, or places kept cool by a constant draught of air, promoted by the disposition and number of the windows; the *calidaria*, where the water was warmed for the baths; the *platanones*, or delightful groves of sycamore; the *stadia*, for the performances of the *athletae*; the *exedrae*, or resting-places, provided with seats for those that were weary; the *palaestrae*, where every one chose that exercise which pleased him best; the *gymnasia*, where poets, orators and philosophers recited their works, and harangued for diversion; the *eleotesia*, where the fragrant oils and ointments were kept for the use of the bathers; and the *conisteria*, where the wrestlers were smeared with sand before they engaged. Of the thermae in Rome, some were mercenary, and some opened gratis. Marcus Agrippa, when he was aedile, opened one hundred and seventy private baths, for the use of the people. In the public baths, where money was taken, each person paid a *quadrans*, about the value of our halfpenny...

Though there was no distinction in the places between the first patrician and the lowest plebeian, yet the nobility used their own silver and gold plate, for washing, eating, and drinking in the bath, together with towels of the finest linen. They likewise made use of the instrument called strigil, which was a kind of flesh-brush...The common people contented themselves with sponges...

There were separate places for the two sexes; and indeed there were baths opened for the use of women only, at the expense of Agrippina, the mother of Nero, and some other matrons of the first quality...In order to preserve decorum in the baths, a set of laws and regulations were published, and the thermae were put under the inspection of a censor, who was generally one of the first senators in Rome.

From *Travels through France and Italy*, 1766

The baths in fiction

Henryk Sienkiewicz sets the first chapter of his *Quo Vadis* in the house of Petronius Arbiter (*see p. 49*). As

Petronius is taking his morning bath he receives a visit from his nephew Marcus Vinicius, who is eager to tell him about a girl he has seen and fallen in love with. Here we join them as they go through the elaborate bathing ritual:

Petronius woke only about midday, and as usual greatly wearied. The evening before he had been at one of Nero's feasts, which was prolonged till late at night. For some time his health had been failing. He said himself that he woke up benumbed, as it were, and without power of collecting his thoughts. But the morning bath and careful kneading of the body by trained slaves hastened gradually the course of his slothful blood, roused him, quickened him, restored his strength, so that he issued from the elaeothesium, that is, the last division of the bath, as if he had risen from the dead...After that feast, at which he was bored by the jesting of Vatinius with Nero, Lucan[2], and Seneca, he took part in a diatribe as to whether woman has a soul. Rising late, he used, as was his custom, the baths. Two enormous balneatores laid him on a cypress table covered with snow-white Egyptian byssus, and with hands dipped in perfumed olive oil began to rub his shapely body;

2 Lucan was a poet, formerly a favourite of Nero but later his enemy. When his involvement in a plot against Nero's life was discovered, he was forced to commit suicide. He was twenty-five.

and he waited with closed eyes till the heat of the la-
conicum[3] and the heat of their hands passed through
him and expelled weariness. But after a certain time
he spoke, and opened his eyes; he inquired about
the weather, and then about gems which the jeweller Idomeneus had promised to send him for ex-
amination that day. It appeared that the weather was
beautiful, with a light breeze from the Alban hills,
and that the gems had not been brought. Petronius
closed his eyes again, and had given command to
bear him to the tepidarium, when from behind the
curtain the nomenclator looked in, announcing that
young Marcus Vinicius, recently returned from Asia
Minor, had come to visit him.

Petronius ordered to admit the guest to the tepidarium, to which he was borne himself. Vinicius
was the son of his oldest sister, who years before had
married Marcus Vinicius[4], a man of consular dignity
from the time of Tiberius. The young man was serving then under Corbulo against the Parthians, and
at the close of the war had returned to the city. Petronius had for him a certain weakness bordering on
attachment, for Marcus was beautiful and athletic,
a young man who knew how to preserve a certain

3 The steam bath.
4 Like Petronius himself, a historical character. He was with Claudius
when he conquered Britain, but was put to death at the urging of the empress Messalina.

aesthetic measure in his profligacy; this, Petronius prized above everything.

'A greeting to Petronius,' said the young man, entering the tepidarium with a springy step. 'May all the gods grant thee success, but especially Aesculapius and Kypris[5], for under their double protection nothing evil can meet one.'

'I greet thee in Rome, and may thy rest be sweet after war,' replied Petronius, extending his hand from between the folds of soft karbas stuff in which he was wrapped. 'What's to be heard in Armenia; or since thou wert in Asia, didst thou not stumble into Bithynia?'

Petronius on a time had been proconsul in Bithynia, and, what is more, he had governed with energy and justice. This was a marvellous contrast in the character of a man noted for effeminacy and love of luxury; hence he was fond of mentioning those times, as they were a proof of what he had been, and of what he might have become had it pleased him.

Vinicius began to talk of the war; but when Petronius closed his eyes again, the young man, seeing his uncle's tired and somewhat emaciated face, changed the conversation, and inquired with a certain interest about his health.

---

5 Aesculapius, Graeco-Roman god of healing. Kypris is Venus, goddess of love and beauty.

Petronius opened his eyes again. Health!—No. He did not feel well. Vinicius had just committed him to the care of Aesculapius and Kypris. But he, Petronius, did not believe in Aesculapius…'As to Kypris…she is a good goddess! I suppose that thou wilt bear sooner or later white doves to her altar.'

'True,' answered Vinicius. 'The arrows of the Parthians have not reached my body, but a dart of Amor has struck me—unexpectedly, a few stadia from a gate of this city.'

'By the white knees of the Graces! Thou wilt tell me of this at a leisure hour.'

'I have come purposely to get thy advice,' answered Marcus.

But at that moment the epilatores came, and occupied themselves with Petronius. Marcus, throwing aside his tunic, entered a bath of tepid water, for Petronius invited him to a plunge bath.

'Ah, I have not even asked whether thy feeling is reciprocated,' said Petronius, looking at the youthful body of Marcus, which was as if cut out of marble. 'Had Lysippus seen thee, thou wouldst be ornamenting now the gate leading to the Palatine, as a statue of Hercules in youth.'

The young man smiled with satisfaction, and began to sink in the bath, splashing warm water abundantly on the mosaic which represented Hera at the moment when she was imploring Sleep to lull Zeus to rest.

Petronius looked at him with the satisfied eye of an artist…

'Hast heard the history of Rufinus?'

'No.'

'Then come to the frigidarium to cool; there I will tell thee.'

They passed to the frigidarium, in the middle of which played a fountain of bright rose colour, emitting the odour of violets. There they sat in niches which were covered with velvet, and began to cool themselves. Silence reigned for a time. Vinicius looked awhile thoughtfully at a bronze faun which, bending over the arm of a nymph, was seeking her lips eagerly with his lips.

'He is right,' said the young man. 'That is what is best in life.'

'More or less! But besides this thou lovest war, for which I have no liking, since under tents one's fingernails break and cease to be rosy…'

'Thou wast to tell me [the history of Rufinus].'

'I will tell it in the unctorium.'

But in the unctorium the attention of Vinicius was turned to other objects; namely, to wonderful slave women who were waiting for the bathers. Two of them, Africans, resembling noble statues of ebony, began to anoint their bodies with delicate perfumes from Arabia; others, Phrygians, skilled in hairdressing, held in their hands, which were bending and flexible as serpents, combs and mirrors of polished steel; two Grecian maidens from Kos, who were simply like deities, waited as *vestiplicae*, till the moment should come to put statuesque folds in the togas of the lords.

'By the cloud-scattering Zeus!' said Marcus Vinicius, 'what a choice thou hast!'

From *Quo Vadis: A Narrative of the Time of Nero*, 1896, Tr, Jeremiah Curtin

George Gissing also writes about the baths in his unfinished novel *Veranilda*, set in Rome in the 6th century. It tells the story of Basil, a Roman, and Veranilda, a Gothic princess and descendant of Theodoric the Great. Here is Basil, mourning the end of the great bath houses in Rome since the cutting of the aqueducts:

George Gissing on the demise of the baths

Vast was the change produced in the Roman's daily existence by the destruction of the aqueducts. The Thermae being henceforth unsupplied with water, those magnificent resorts of every class of citizen lost their attraction, and soon ceased to be frequented; for all the Roman's exercises and amusements were associated with the practice of luxurious bathing, and without that refreshment the gymnasium, the tennis-court, the lounge, no longer charmed as before. Rome became dependent upon wells and the Tiber, wretched resource compared with the never-failing and abundant streams which once poured through every region of the city and threw up fountains in all but every street. Belisarius, as soon as the Goths retreated, ordered the repairing of an aqueduct, that which served the transtiberine district, and was indispensable to the working of the Janiculan mills, where corn was ground; but, after his departure, there was neither enough energy nor sufficient sense of security in Rome for the restoration of even one of the greater conduits. Nobles and populace alike lived without the bath, grew accustomed to more or less uncleanliness, and in a certain quarter suffered worse than inconvenience from the lack of good water.

Formerly a young Roman of Basil's rank, occupied or not by any serious pursuit, would have spent several hours of the day at one or other of the Thermae still in use; if inclined to display, he would have gone thither with a train of domestic attendants, and probably of parasites; were the season hot, here he found coolness; were it cold, here he warmed himself. Society never failed; opportunity for clandestine meetings could always be found; all the business and the pleasure of a day were regulated with reference to this immemorial habit. Now, to enter the Thermae was to hear one's footsteps resound in a marble wilderness; to have statues for companions and a sense of ruin for one's solace...

From *Veranilda*, 1903

One of the most famous water features in Rome, on every visitor's list of things that must be seen, experienced, and—in our own day—photographed, is the Trevi Fountain. It was traditionally admired more as a phenomenon than as a work of art. Shelley damns it with faint praise (*see p. 251*) and it was not generally admired as sculpture: Nathaniel Hawthorne talks about the sculptor having 'gone absolutely mad in marble'. Its fame as a means to ensure a return to Rome, by tossing a coin into it over one's shoulder, is well known and still honoured (the coins are periodically collected and given to charity).

On tossing a coin into the Trevi Fountain

In tears I tossed my coin from Trevi's edge,—
  A coin unsordid as a bond of love,—
  And, with the instinct of the homing dove,
I gave to Rome my rendezvous and pledge.
    And when imperious Death
    Has quenched my flame of breath,
Oh, let me join the faithful shades that throng that
  fount above.

Robert Underwood Johnson, 1917

THE AUTHORS

Short biographical details of all the writers quoted at length in this anthology are given here, in alphabetical order.

Hans Christian Andersen (1805–75): The son of a poor Danish shoemaker and a simple, superstitious mother, Andersen was sent to school partly through the beneficence of others. His schooldays were unhappy but his love of literature and the theatre remained with him. Today he is chiefly known for his children's stories, among them *The Ugly Duckling* and *The Emperor's New Clothes*. Andersen travelled widely. *The Improvisatore*, written in Rome, was his first novel. Though he fell in love many times, his feelings were always unrequited and he never married.

Apuleius (2nd century BC): Prose writer and scholar from Roman Numidia, modern Algeria. Many of the themes in his *Metamorphoses* or *The Golden Ass* are taken from life—he was accused of having recourse to witchcraft and the speech he made in self-defence still survives. Apuleius was widely travelled and was an initiate of a number of religious cults.

Benjamin of Tudela: Nothing at all is known of the life of Benjamin, except that he was a native of Tudela in Navarre,

Spain, and that between about 1159 and 1172 he travelled around the Mediterranean and into Arabia. His diaries of the journey are an important source work for the period.

Bernard Berenson (1865–1959): Berenson was born in Lithuania, the son of parents who emigrated to Boston, Massachusetts. On graduating from Harvard he travelled to Europe, funded by the Boston art collector Isabella Stewart Gardner. Europe was to be Berenson's home for the rest of his life. His plans to write a novel came to nothing; instead he fashioned himself into the most influential art historian and critic of the first half of the 20th century. *The Passionate Sightseer*, published posthumously in 1960, is a collection of entries from his diaries between 1947 and 1956.

James Boswell (1740–95): Scottish writer, most famous for his *Life of Samuel Johnson*. He was also a great traveller, and has left accounts of many of his journeys, both in Britain and abroad. Always of an amorous disposition (with Boswell, in fact, it was pathological), he is candid about his brief encounters and his battles with venereal disease.

Elizabeth Bowen (1899–1973): Anglo-Irish writer, one of the great novelists of the 1930s. Her prose beautifully examines the lives that boil and bubble under a surface of calm respectability—her own life was one of marital contentment and extra-marital liaison. *A Time in Rome* is an excellent introduction to the city, both ancient and modern, written unabashedly for readers who have not spent their lives studying the Classics. As Bowen says of herself, 'I have no Latin'.

Robert Browning (1812–89): Though Browning began his poetic career as an imitator of Byron and Shelley, he quickly relinquished the style, being temperamentally unsuited to it: he was, in fact, profoundly 'normal' and 'Victorian'. His great talent was for poetry as drama; and Italy, where he lived for much of his life, provided him with a rich cast of characters. He made his name with the voluminous *Ring and the Book*, which tells the true story, from different points of view, of a murder trial in 17th-century Rome.

Charles Burney (1726–1814): Composer and musical historian. He toured Europe in 1770, gathering material for his *History of Music*. He was the father of the novelist Fanny Burney.

Lord Byron (1788–1824): George Gordon Byron was the most famous poet of his age, feeding a public that was as agog to know the scandals of his private life as it was to peruse his verses. When in Rome on tour he became enamoured of the *Apollo Belvedere* and even, it is said, began to model his own appearance on the statue. His public and poetic personae are well known: aristocratic rebel, untameable libertine, champion of the underdog, show-off.

Even his friend Shelley despaired of Byron's posturing. Of *Childe Harold* he said, 'The spirit in which it is written is, if insane, the most wicked and mischievous insanity that was ever given forth'; and of the company he kept, that 'He associates with wretches who seem almost to have lost the gait and physiognomy of man'.

John Capgrave (1393–1464): English Augustinian friar and theologian. His writings include biblical commentaries, hagiographies and a life of his patron, Humphrey, Duke of Gloucester (who left many books in his will to the Bodleian Library in Oxford). After a visit to Rome in 1449–50, Capgrave wrote *Ye Solace of Pilgrimes*, at once a visitors' guide and a book of anecdotes about the city and its sights.

Thomas Carlyle (1795–1881): The life of Thomas Carlyle is a superb illustration of the social mobility of late Georgian Britain. Born the son of a poor Scottish stonemason, he rose to be lionised as 'the sage of Chelsea'. Carlyle had intended himself for the Kirk but a crisis of faith prevented it, and he earned a living instead as a tutor, writing on the side. In 1834 he moved to London and made his name with *The French Revolution: A History*. In later life he became more and more reactionary, a believer in resolute, even ruthless, leadership. This is the subject of *On Heroes and Hero-Worship*.

Cato the Censor (2nd century BC): Marcus Porcius Cato was a Roman soldier and politician of the late Republic. Famed for an ascetic nature and a conservative stance, he was the model of the old Roman, a man who served loyally in the army when required, and when war was at and end would return to his farm to till the soil. He abhorred all forms of luxury and was a political enemy of Scipio Africanus, whom he considered extravagant and a bad influence on the troops. In 184 he was appointed censor, and was notorious for his strictness, expelling a man from the senate for the crime of embracing his wife in public in the presence of their daughter.

Catullus (1st century BC): Gaius Valerius Catullus, from a well-to-do family of Verona, spent most of his adulthood in Rome, where he wrote his now famous verses. These are by turns tender and obscene, written in language that makes schoolboy Latin students titter, filled with slurs on prominent figures (Caesar and Cicero) and with alternate praise and invective directed at the woman he calls Lesbia. Catullus died young, perhaps before his thirtieth birthday.

Benvenuto Cellini (1500–71): Florentine goldsmith and sculptor whose famous *Autobiography* reveals his talents not only as a fine artist but also as a soldier, musician, ladies' man and raconteur. He was in Rome in 1527, when the city was sacked by the troops of the Holy Roman Emperor.

Claire Clairmont (1798–1879): Stepsister of Mary Shelley and companion to both Shelleys on their continental travels (many have suspected that the three enjoyed some sort of *ménage à trois*). A brief affair with Byron resulted in a daughter, Allegra, who was placed in Byron's care and died in an Italian convent at the age of five. In later life Clairmont worked as a music teacher, governess and ladies' companion. She returned to Italy in her last years and (with papers of Shelley's in her possession) was the inspiration for the character of Juliana Bordereau in Henry James' *The Aspern Papers*.

Arthur Hugh Clough (1819–61): The leitmotifs of Clough's life and work are unfulfilled promise, indecision, paralysis of will, crisis of faith. Clough was also interested in political upheaval; he witnessed revolutions in France and Italy. By nature philanthropic (his wife, incidentally, was related to Florence Nightingale), he had a keen sense of not having done as well as he could or should. The title of his most famous poem, *Say Not the Struggle Naught Availeth*, sums it up.

Charles Dickens (1812–70): By the time he came to publish *Pictures from Italy* in 1846, Dickens was a household name, with some of his most famous novels (*Oliver Twist*, *Nicholas Nickleby*) already behind him. Essentially *Pictures* is a famous man's travelogue, and it reads as such. His descriptions of Italy are nevertheless revealing, not only about the country as it then was, but also about Dickens himself. His love of the theatre and spectacle comes out strongly, as well as his fundamental qualities of humanity and compassion.

Cassius Dio (2nd–3rd centuries AD): Roman historian of Greek ancestry (he wrote in Greek) who held various public appointments across the Empire. His *Roman History* begins with the mythical arrival of Aeneas from Troy and continues up to real events from the author's own lifetime. Scholars argue about his style and methods; the great value for the ordinary reader lies in the fact that Dio actually lived through much of what he wrote about.

George Eliot (1819–80): Victorian sentimentality and a fierce intellect are allied in the novels of George Eliot (Mary Ann Evans), who criticised the works of Dickens (who had the former but not the latter) and Jane Austen (who had neither, but was funny and was content with happy endings). Eliot is concerned with questions of faith and religion, social reform, morality and the position of women (she herself lived with a married man who was unable to obtain a divorce). *Middlemarch: A Study of Provincial Life* is considered her masterpiece. She wrote only six other novels, believing that 'excessive literary production is a social offence'.

Erasmus (1466–1536): Desiderius Erasmus, the Dutch theologian and humanist, was one of the greatest Church scholars of his day. He was widely travelled and lived variously in England, the Low Countries, Italy and Switzerland. Though his name is often associated with the Protestant Reformation, his position always remained ambiguous. When accused of 'laying the egg that Luther hatched,' he is reputed to have replied that he had 'expected a different bird'.

John Evelyn (1620–1706): The diarist John Evelyn entered the English Civil War on the Royalist side but soon afterwards obtained permission to leave for the Continent, because he was reluctant to do 'very unhandsome things'. It was then that he saw Rome. His descriptions are closely-observed and interesting, never salacious (unlike those of his contemporary, Samuel Pepys). Evelyn was also a great horticulturalist, a founder of the Royal Society, a patron of the arts and a loving husband and father.

Edward Gibbon (1737–94): Gibbon showed little promise as a young man. He failed to take a degree at Oxford, converted to Catholicism and then back again, fell in love with a woman his father deemed unsuitable (she married another and was the mother of Madame de Staël)—and finally embarked on the Grand Tour. This was the making of him. 'It was at Rome,' he famously declared, 'on the 15th of October 1764, as I sat musing amidst the ruins of the Capitol, while the bare-footed friars were singing vespers in the temple of Jupiter, that the idea of writing the decline and fall of the city first started to my mind.' That *Decline and Fall*, published in 1776–88, remains one of the greatest history books ever written in the English language.

George Gissing (1857–1903): Though gifted and hard-working, Gissing's life was dogged by poverty and personal unhappiness and his novels only enjoyed a moderate success. Gissing's social conscience was strong. His first wife was an alcoholic whom he tried to redeem from prostitution; his second was a street-girl whom he attempted, Pygmalion-like, to educate. She was mentally unstable and was later placed in an asylum. In his works his favourite theme is the plight of the working poor. After seeing the dead body of his first wife in a London slum, he wrote 'Henceforth I never cease to bear testimony against the accursed social order that brings about things of this kind'. With the money he made from one of his books he visited Rome, a city he had always longed to see. *Veranilda* was his last novel, left unfinished at the time of his death, from emphysema.

Goethe (1749–1832): Johann Wolfgang von Goethe, the greatest writer in the German language, was at once a poet, dramatist, novelist, amateur scientist and philosopher, and has been one of the most influential figures in all of European literature. His mature oeuvre brings together the Gothic north and the Classical south, a fusion which took place in his consciousness after his visit to Italy, a country where he finally came alive after an existence of servitude to a master (the court of Weimar) and a mistress (the older, married, difficult Charlotte von Stein). When he arrived in Rome in 1786, Goethe exclaimed, 'Only now do I begin to live!'

Robert Graves (1895–1985): Poet of the Great War, later also a novelist and translator from the Classics. His successful novel *I, Claudius*, written as if it were the emperor's own autobiography, together with its sequel, *Claudius the God*, were successfully adapted for television.

Thomas Gray (1716–71): A Classical scholar and poet in the Augustan tradition, Gray was born into a very humble family. The only one of his many siblings to survive infancy, he was a sensitive character and enjoyed a close relationship with his mother. At school he made friends with the patrician and robust Horace Walpole and they went on a European tour together, which is when Gray saw Rome. Gray's poems can be academic and too crowded with allusions, only really understandable with extensive footnotes. His most famous are the light-hearted elegy on the death of Walpole's cat and the heavier-hearted *Elegy in a Country Churchyard*.

Ferdindand Gregorovius (1821–91): German historian, the son of a Lutheran minister. Like Gibbon before him, Gregorovius received the idea to write his history in a Damascene flash: it was in 1854, as he stood on a bridge over the Tiber. The resulting *History of the City of Rome in the Middle Ages* has never been surpassed, though Gregorovius was not an academic and university men have crowed over the errors in it. Gregorovius' Rome was that of Pope Pius IX, whose troubled papacy was battling for its political life against the revolutionary forces of Italian nationalism. The battle was lost just one year before Gregorovius finished writing. 'The idea of the work,' he said, 'was suggested by the overwhelming spectacle of the monumental grandeur of the city, and perhaps by the presentiment which made itself obscurely felt at the time, that the history of the Roman Middle Ages would soon reach its perfect close in the downfall of the papal dominion.'

Thomas Hardy (1840–1928): Poet and novelist associated in most people's minds with rural Dorset, England. In 1887, however, Hardy undertook a tour of Europe, and he expressed what he saw in *Poems of Pilgrimage*. The four poems he wrote in Rome all explore the way the ancient past wreathes its ghostly power around the insistent present.

Augustus Hare (1834–1903): English writer, born in Rome. His writings are mainly either autobiography and family history or travel books.

Nathaniel Hawthorne (1804–64): Born in Salem, Massachusetts, of Puritan stock, an ancestry that makes itself felt in his novels, most famously *The Scarlet Letter*. But in *The Marble Faun*, too, we are perpetually reminded that Hilda is a 'daughter of Puritans'. Hawthorne and his family travelled to Europe in 1857, where they remained for three years and where Hawthorne grew his moustache. On his return to America he published *The Marble Faun*, which enjoyed considerable success.

William Hazlitt (1778–1830): Chiefly known as a political essayist, Hazlitt led a hand-to-mouth existence for most of his life, frantically writing to pay the bills. He knew many of the leading writers of the day, including Words-worth and Coleridge, but his tactless, irascible style caused him to quarrel with them. In 1824, accompanied by his second wife, he embarked on a tour of Europe, which included Rome. The city did not particularly impress him; his real love was Paris, the city of his idol, Napoleon.

John Cam Hobhouse (1786–1869): Hobhouse befriended Byron at Cambridge and travelled with him to Greece. He wrote the annotations to the Fourth Canto of *Childe Harold*, which Byron dedicated to him. In later life he turned to radical politics, becoming MP for Westminster in 1820. He was created Baron Broughton in 1851.

Richard Holmes (b. 1945): Holmes's biography of Shelley, *The Pursuit*, won the Somerset Maugham Award in 1974. *Footsteps* is part-autobiography, part-travelogue, insightful and entertaining notes of an author's adventures in the footsteps of his subjects, Robert Louis Stevenson, Gautier, Wordsworth, Shelley and Gérard de Nerval, through France and Italy.

Lord Houghton (1809–85): Richard Monckton Miles, 1st Baron Houghton, was a friend of Tennyson and an admirer (and ultimately rejected suitor) of Florence Nightingale. He surrounded himself with a literary circle and wrote poetry of his own. Mainly, however, he is known as a patron of other writers, instrumental in furthering the career of Swinburne.

Horace (1st century BC): Quintus Horatius Flaccus was the son of a wealthy freedman who paid for his son to receive an education at Rome and Athens. Horace fought alongside Brutus at the Battle of Philippi, and by his own admission deserted the field. Later he was pardoned by Augustus, who commissioned a number of verses from him. His treatise on poetry, the *Ars Poetica*, was greatly influential on poets of the modern era. Lest we should imagine him as a noble-minded scholar, it is worth considering that a contemporary source described him as short, fat and intemperate in his lusts.

Edward Hutton (1875–1969): Hutton is best known as a writer on art history and travel, particularly relating to Italy. He was a founder of the British Institute of Florence. During the Second World War he helped the British Foreign Office protect works from damage and destruction.

Jean Auguste Dominique Ingres (1780–1867): French painter in the Neoclassical tradition, best known today for his portraits. He came to Rome to study in 1806, and while there received news of how badly his works had been received at the Paris Salon. It was not until almost 20 years later that his painting received public recognition, and even then the praise was not unanimous. The orientalist fashion for voluptuous studies of bathers and odalisques helped somewhat to establish him, but largely it has been left to posterity to create his reputation.

Henry James (1843–1916): One of the great 19th-century American novelists, a consummate stylist and enthusiastic admirer of Europe, where he spent much of his life, largely in Italy and England (he became a British citizen in 1915). The protagonists of many of his works are Americans abroad, and one of his favourite themes is the clash between the childlike innocence or naivety of the New World and the sophistication (good and bad) of the old. Many of his central characters are women, his plots are largely connected with the question of who is going to marry whom, and modern critics, in an age when everyone is required to have a sexual orientation, have speculated endlessly over James's. His writing is always rather sober: one does not tend to think of him as a great drinker. Yet a letter sent from Rome by his brother William in 1873, addressed to their sister, remarks on his own abstinence from 'spiritous liquors, to which Harry, I regret to say, has become an utter slave, spending a large part of his earnings in Bass's Ale and wine, and trembling with anger if there is any delay in their being brought to him'.

Robert Underwood Johnson (1853–1937): Journalist, poet and diplomat: Johnson's career culminated in his appointment as US Ambassador to Italy. During an earlier visit to the country in 1917 he had written his *Italian Rhapsody and Other*

Poems. He was instrumental in the move to buy the house where Keats died and to set it up as a museum.

Juvenal (1st–2nd centuries AD): Decimus Junius Juvenalis was a satiric poet, best known for his portrayal of life in Rome. He is thought to have been the son of a freedman, to have pursued a career as a jurist, and to have turned to poetry late in life.

John Keats (1795–1821): Keats was something of an outsider among the English Romantic poets, most of whom came from well-to-do backgrounds. Keats was the son of a London ostler. Originally he planned to become a surgeon, but gave up medicine to devote himself to poetry. Consumption ran in the family. It claimed his mother and one of his brothers before making itself manifest in Keats too. In 1820 his physician prescribed a drier climate and Keats set off for Italy. At about the same time his poems began to receive favourable notices—but for Keats it was too late. He died in Rome the following February.

Jhumpa Lahiri (b. 1967): Lahiri was born in London, to Bengali parents, and grew up in the United States. She won the Pulitzer Prize for her first collection of stories, *Interpreter of Maladies*. The main theme of her work is how people cope with being caught between two cultures.

Edward Lear (1812–88): Lear's first ambition was to be a

painter. He was a gifted landscape artist and
painter of birds and animals. He came to Rome
through the generosity of his patron, the Earl
of Derby, and attempted, unsuccessfully, to
make a living by his art. The optimism of his
early letters quickly gives way to disappointment. After Rome
Lear embarked on a series of lengthy travels. He eventually
settled in Italy. Fame never came to him in the way he wished.
Instead he became known for his nonsense verse.

Carlo Levi (1902–75): Born in Turin into a family with
socialist political affiliations, Levi trained as a doctor but
made his name as a journalist, writer, painter and political
activist. His outspoken anti-Fascism led to his arrest in 1934
and he was sent into political exile in Basilicata. The divide
in Italy between rich and poor, developed and undeveloped,
privileged and deprived, became a preoccupation in his writing ever afterwards. Always involved in politics, he was elected to the Italian senate in 1963. He died in Rome.

Helen MacInnes (1907–85): Scottish-born writer famous
for her spy novels set in beautiful, historic or exotic locations.
She moved to the United States in 1937, becoming an American citizen in 1951.

Martial (1st–2nd centuries AD): Marcus Valerius Martialis was
the author of the *Epigrams*, short satirical poems about Rome
and its inhabitants. Essentially commentaries on social life,

they are by turns scurrilous, cynical, humorous and toady-ing—particularly with regard to emperors whose favour Mari-tal wished to court. He was successful and well known in his lifetime, but always hard-up.

John Milton (1608–71): Poet, Puritan and supporter of the Parliamentarians in the English Civil War, Milton's fame rests on his great poem *Paradise Lost*. After leaving university, he immersed himself in a programme of study, part of which involved a tour of France and Italy. He spent two months in Rome, viewing the antiquities and impressing local poets with his erudition.

Montaigne (1533–92): The great French essayist and thinker Michel de Montaigne came to Rome in 1580–81. For a long time it had occupied a central place in his imagi-nation. 'I used all my five senses of nature to obtain the title of Roman citizen,' he tells us, 'if only for the ancient honour and religious memory of its au-thority.' The honour was granted him by Pope Gregory XIII.

J.B.S. Morritt (1771–1843): John Bacon Sawrey Morritt in-herited his father's estate at the age of twenty-two. He promptly set off on the Grand Tour, and on his return settled into Roke-by Park in Yorkshire, which he proceeded to embellish with cultivated taste. His most famous acquisition was Velázquez's *Rokeby Venus* (now in the National Gallery, London). He describes hanging it in an amusing letter to his friend Sir Walter Scott: 'I have been all morning pulling about my pictures and hanging them in new positions to make more room for my fine picture of Venus' backside by Velasquez which I have at length exalted over my chimney piece in the library. It is an admirable light for the painting, and shows it in perfection, whilst by raising the said backside to a considerable height the ladies may avert their downcast eyes without difficulty, and connoisseurs steal a glance without drawing in the said posterior as a part of the company.' The painting annoyed early feminists. It was slashed by a furious suffragette in 1914.

Axel Munthe (1857–1949): Swedish doctor and writer, author of the famous *Story of San Michele*, which not only tells the tale of the author's villa at Anacapri but also describes his life and work in Paris, Rome and Naples. Munthe's speciality was psychiatry, particularly the treatment of female hysteria. He was interested in alternative routes towards healing, such as music therapy or hypnosis. He was a humane man, a lover of animals and a believer in euthanasia, and was known for his dispensation of free medical aid to those who could not pay. His writings are filled with sad tales of desperate people, poor and ill and on the margins of society.

Ouida (1839–1908): Maria Louisa Ramé chose the pen-name Ouida after the way she had pronounced her middle name as a child ('Weeda'). She began writing at an early age, and throughout her life produced an indefatigable string of terrible novels. She was mad about dogs, and a Maltese terrier appears as narrator in one of them. What she lacks in literary merit she makes up for in enthusiastic self-belief. In 1874 she moved to Italy, remaining there for the rest of her life.

Ovid (43 BC–AD 17 or 18): Publius Ovidius Naso, a poet of the age of Augustus, is best known for his *Metamorphoses* (a retelling of Classical myths) and for his poems on the art of love and seduction. Popular and influential in his own lifetime, he was exiled to the Black Sea for reasons that remain obscure, and died far from his beloved Rome.

William Patoun (d. 1783): Painter, dilettante and member of the Florence Accademia. Piranesi dedicated a drawing to him in his *Vasi ed Ornamenti Antichi*. According to his obituary in *The Gentleman's Magazine*, 'to the most amiable manners and the most perfect integrity and virtue, he joined great learning and a thorough knowledge of the fine arts. He had attained an uncommon degree of excellence in painting and music; was an adept in chemistry, and had made some important discoveries and improvements in colours, which, we hope, will not be lost to the public.'

Petronius (d. AD 66): When Beau Nash nominated himself *arbiter elegantiarum* of Regency Bath he was taking Petronius as his model. Known as Petronius 'Arbiter', this consummate courtier acted as Nero's referee on all matters of elegance, taste and fashion. His power was good while it lasted. Tacitus informs us that Petronius spent his days sleeping and his nights having fun, that he turned idleness to profit and luxury into an art. His eventual downfall was the work of a rival, who poisoned Nero's mind against him. Like Seneca before him, Petronius committed suicide by bleeding himself to death—but even that final act he performed with nonchalance and style. He was probably (but not certainly) the author of the *Satyricon*, a sometimes amusing, often disgusting, satire from the days of depravity that were Nero's reign.

Edgar Allan Poe (1800–49): Poet and story-writer, the father of the psychological thriller. Poe's was a troubled life, a story of penury, alcoholism and early death. Nevertheless he has gained a reputation as one of the foremost men of American letters.

Peter Porter (1929–2010): Australian-born poet resident in England from 1955 to his death. His own description of the contemporary poet's task remains the clearest way to summarise the character of his work: 'the best of the old discipline with the best of the new freedom of expression'.

Mario Praz (1892–1982): Critic and professor of literature in his native Italy and in England, Praz was the author of *The Romantic Agony*, a study of the literature of the Romantic age. He also wrote a history of interior design. *The House of*

Life takes the reader on an intimate and detailed tour of his Roman apartment near Piazza Navona (it is now a museum).

Propertius (1st century BC): Details of Propertius' life are obscure (we do not even know his full name), but he seems to have followed some kind of public career in Rome, coming to the attention of the great patron of the arts, Maecenas, on the publication of his first poems. Love and its tribulations are his principal themes.

Barbara Pym (1913–80): 'Of course it is all right for librarians to smell of drink.' The image that that line conjures up—of loneliness, escapism, genteel destitution and the yearning for something more—is the quintessence of Pym's writing and of her humour. During the Second World War she joined the Women's Royal Naval Service and was posted to Italy.

Francisco de Quevedo (1580–1645): One of the most important figures of the so-called Golden Century of Spanish literature, a rival of Góngora. In 1613 he was sent on a diplomatic mission to Italy. When his political career and his marriage failed, he retired to his estates in La Mancha.

Frederick Rolfe (1860–1913): Self-centred, suspicious, ungrateful and vainglorious are not adjectives which paint a very endearing picture: Frederick Rolfe was not a likeable man, nor an honest one. He styled himself 'Baron Corvo', claiming that he had received the title from a Roman countess. A Catholic convert, he took to signing his name 'Fr. Rolfe', as though a man of the cloth, though his vocation to the priesthood had been frustrated by expulsion from his seminary. Rolfe was a fantasist, convinced of his own superiority: of spirit, intellect and as a writer. In *Hadrian the Seventh* an Englishman, George Rose (a thinly-disguised Rolfe) is elected pope, and zealously embarks on the task of reforming the Catholic world. Rolfe had few friends (he sponged off those he had and then betrayed their generosity by lampooning them in his writing) and never had a lasting love affair. In the words of the Penguin potted biography, he found 'an outlet for his tangled emotions in extensive pederasty'. He died destitute in Venice.

John Ruskin (1819–1900): An influential writer on art and architecture, John Ruskin was mostly self-taught and belonged to no school of thought; his mind was too independent and too original. He was consciously and deliberately old-fashioned, even fusty, in his views and his mode of expression; but also—less consciously but more interestingly—very modern: he saw architecture as a tool for social improvement and is credited with providing the intellectual basis for the foundation of the British Labour Party. His great love was the Gothic, which he saw as hand-made, craftsmanlike and reflecting the genius of individual artisans. The Renaissance for him was imitative, decadent and ungodly.

Seneca (d. AD 65). Lucius Annaeus Seneca, author of the famous *Moral Epistles*, was a Stoic philosopher and writer who served as advisor to the unstable and megalomaniac emperor Nero. When implicated (probably falsely) in a plot to kill the emperor, he was ordered to commit suicide.

Percy Bysshe Shelley (1792–1822): Shelley is one of the most famous of the English Romantic poets, for some a cult figure. Scandals in his private life (his first wife committed suicide) and his personal beliefs (free love, vegetarianism, atheism) and attaching to his poetry (the portrayal of incestuous love) meant that he was never accepted in establishment circles. His last years were spent in Italy; he was a contemporary and friend of Byron. After the death of Keats, whom he had known slightly, he wrote the elegy *Adonaïs*. He drowned when his boat sank off Livorno, and his body was cremated on the beach. His heart, snatched from the pyre, was interred in the Protestant Cemetery in Rome. Shelley was never successful or widely read in his lifetime. Popularity came only after his death.

Henryk Sienkiewicz (1846–1916): Polish novelist, chiefly of historical subjects, often with a proud patriotic flavour. *Quo Vadis* was his greatest international success. He was awarded the Nobel Prize for Literature in 1905.

Tobias Smollett (1721–71): Scottish-born writer best known for two picaresque novels, *The Adventures of Roderick Random* and *The*

Adventures of Humphrey Clinker. He travelled to the continent with his wife following the death of their daughter, and published *Travels through France and Italy* in 1766. He returned to Italy in his last years and died at Livorno.

Madame de Staël (1766–1817): Anne Louise Germaine de Staël was born in Paris to Swiss parents. Her father was Jacques Necker, Louis XIV's finance minister. Intensely intellectual, her salon became one of the most influential of its day. She began publishing novels at the age of 20. Her husband was a Swedish diplomat. It was a marriage of convenience—chiefly for him, for his bride had brains and a fortune. When the French Revolution broke out, de Staël escaped to Switzerland. Her political views (she believed in constitutional government) later brought her into conflict with Napoleon. According to James Parton (in *Daughters of Genius: A Series of Sketches of authors, artists, reformers, and heroines, queens, princesses, and women of society, women eccentric and peculiar*, Philadelphia, 1886), while Napoleon was 'dazzling and intoxicating France…the woman would not be dazzled. In a city delirious she kept her senses. In a company drunk, she remained sober'. She travelled to Italy after her father's death in 1804, and wrote *Corinne* on her return.

Stendhal (1783–1842): Marie-Henri Beyle, who took the pen-name Stendhal, served in Napoleon's army in 1812 and moved to Italy following Napoleon's exile to Elba two years later. He spent much of the rest of his life there, and it was in Italy that he wrote one of his greatest novels, *The Charterhouse of Parma*.

William Wetmore Story (1819–95): Story graduated from Harvard Law School, intending to follow his father into the legal profession. He gave it up, however, and took up sculpture, and after 1850 spent all of his time in Italy, chiefly Rome, where he was a popular member of the expatriate community (the 'American Village', as Henry James called it). Story was also a poet, novelist and essayist. Henry James wrote his biography, though he had a low opinion of Story's sculpture. 'There is nothing for me but to leave poor W.W.S. *out*, practically,' he said. The book turned out more a description of Italy. Nathaniel Hawthorne describes one of Story's most famous sculptures, *Cleopatra*, in his *Marble Faun*. Story is buried in Rome, in the Protestant Cemetery.

Algernon Charles Swinburne (1837–1909): Aesthete and poet, a devotee of the Pre-Raphaelites, with all that conjures up of medievalism and sentimental fantasy. He enjoyed posing as a hopeless decadent, though many (including, famously, Oscar Wilde) have doubted how far he was really steeped in vice. He certainly had a penchant for the drink. He was passionately wedded to the cause of Italian unity. In poetry he has been called a 'technician'. Many have admired his facility with complicated rhymes and metres. Sometimes, however, the effect is too contrived.

Tacitus (1st–2nd centuries AD): The Roman Empire adopted, co-opted and assimilated men of talent from many conquered lands. Martial was Iberian by birth, Cassius Dio was from Bithynia, Apuleius from Numidia. Cornelius Tacitus is thought to have been from Gaul. Like so many Latin writers, he pursued a public career, as senator, consul and provincial governor. He studied oratory in Rome and embarked on his writing career in the late 1st century. The *Annals* cover the period from the death of Augustus (AD 14) to the death of Nero (AD 68).

Raleigh Trevelyan (b. 1923): Trevelyan served in Italy in the Second World War. His first book, *The Fortress: A Diary of Anzio and After* (1956), is now a classic of its genre.

Mark Twain (1835–1910): The early life of Samuel Langhorne Clemens was exceptionally adventurous: he formed a Confederate militia at the outbreak of the Civil War, panned for gold in Nevada, wrote for newspapers in San Francisco and worked on the Mississippi. If is from this last that he derived his pen-name: 'Mark Twain' is the mark on a depth-sounding rope indicating a depth of two fathoms, deep enough for a steamer. Twain turned all that he had seen and done into source material for his novels. Before he turned to novel-writing he toured the Mediterranean on the SS *Quaker City*. The result was a series of articles on the ship's progress, with satirical descriptions of his fellow passengers. It was published as a compilation entitled *The Innocents Abroad or the New Pilgrim's Progress* (1869), and became a best-seller. In later life Twain became melancholy and misanthropic. In his short story *The Capitoline Venus*, the seeds of cynicism about human nature are there, but the wit and sparkle have not yet departed. The story is based on a real event, the unearthing of a 'petrified giant' in New York, which turned out to be a hoax.

Varro (116–27 BC). Marcus Terentius Varro had an early political career under Pompey, commanding an army against Julius Caesar. He was pardoned and returned to favour. Augustus was also lenient to him, and he devoted the rest of his life to scholarship and writing. His output was large, encompassing many subjects, and many later writers used him as a source.

Edith Wharton (1862–1937): New York-born writer whose works wittily and often bleakly dissect the privileged, aimless lives of the class into which she was born. An unhappy marriage and an unsuccessful love affair largely inform her attitude to relations between the sexes. Wharton travelled widely in Europe (she later settled in France) and was a friend of Henry James. She was the first woman to win the Pulitzer Prize for literature, despite early problems with publishers' censors. Of the polarised nature of the reading public's tastes she remarked caustically, 'half the morons yell for filth, and the other half continue to put pants on the piano-legs'.

Thornton Wilder (1897–1975): Novelist and playwright, born in Wisconsin. After obtaining a masters degree in French from Princeton, he studied in Rome, and during the Second World War worked for US Air Force Intelligence in Italy. Wilder won three Pulitzer prizes, one of them for his best-known work, *The Bridge of San Luis Rey*. His play *The Matchmaker* was adapted to become the hit musical *Hello, Dolly!*. *The Ides of March* is a recreation (with some historic licence) of the Rome of 45 BC, primarily serving as a portrait of Julius Caesar, the dictator who foresees his own death.

William Wordsworth (1770–1850): One of the great English Romantic poets, an early supporter of the French Revolution (though after the Terror he changed his mind). In 1825, without ever having visited Rome, he wrote a long poem about Trajan's Column as an example to his son of what could be done purely by gleaning from books. Wordsworth finally saw Rome in 1837. 'It is not particular objects that make the glory of this city,' he wrote to his sister Dorothy, 'but the boundless variety of combinations old and new'.

GENERAL INDEX

Authors of major quoted extracts, whose biographies appear on pp. 267–94, are given in capitals. Bold type is used to indicate major quoted extracts. Translators are indicated by (Tr.). Titles of works quoted from are given in italics. A separate index of the sights and monuments described in the extracts begins on p. 302.

Adlington, William (Tr.) 129

Adonaïs 222–23

Advice to a Nobleman 8–10

Amours de Voyage 24–25, 153–56

ANDERSEN, HANS CHRISTIAN 41, 63, **149–50, 203–05**, 267

Angela, Alberto 20

Apollo Belvedere, statue 167, 269

APULEIUS **126–29**, 267

Ariadne: The Story of a Dream 161–63

Arnold, Thomas 7

Ars Amatoria 236

Asher, Adolf (Tr.) 55

Atrium of the Vestals 245, 247

Augustus, emperor 100–02,

231, 232, 235, 237ff, 279

A Very Private Eye 140

Baths 254–65

Baths of Caracalla 183, 254, 255

Baths of Diocletian 254

Beckwith, Charles (Tr.) 150

Bembo, Pietro 110

BENJAMIN OF TUDELA **53–55**, 267

Bennett, Charles E. (Tr.) 249

BERENSON, BERNARD 102, 182, **183–84**, 268

Borghese Gallery 171

Borghese Gardens 43–45

BOSWELL, JAMES **241–42**, 268

BOWEN, ELIZABETH **47–48**, **245–48**, 268

Brodribb, William Jackson (Tr.)

116

BROWNING, ROBERT 171, 210, **211–13**, 269

BURNEY, CHARLES **120–22**, 269

Byres, James 9

BYRON, LORD 83, **85–87**, 93, 269, 272

Caffè Greco 62, 163

Campo de' Fiori 59

CAPGRAVE, JOHN **189–91**, 270

Capitoline Hill 17, 38, 100, 187–88, 274

Capitoline Venus, statue 167, 177

Capitoline Venus, The, short story 172–76

Capuchin church 199–205

CARLYLE, THOMAS **141–42**, 270

Carnival 65–70, 187, 215

Cary, Earnest (Tr.) 82

CASSIUS DIO **81–82**, 273

Castel Sant'Angelo 150, 151–53

Catacombs 205–08

Catiline 106

CATO THE CENSOR 71, 228, **229–31**, 270–71

CATULLUS **243**, 270

CELLINI, BENVENUTO **151–53**, **178–80**, 271

Cestius, Pyramid of 34, 221

Chaucer, Geoffrey 7

Childe Harold's Pilgrimage 85, 270

Church, Alfred John (Tr.) 116

CLAIRMONT, CLAIRE **42**, 271–72

Clement VII, pope 150, 152

CLOUGH, ARTHUR HUGH 23, **24–25**, **153–56**, 272

Colosseum 78–95

Constantine, emperor 98; (Arch of) 105–06; (Donation of) 147

Corinne, ou L'Italie 38–41

Corso 65, 67, 68, 70, 158, 165, 187

Corvo, Baron (*see Rolfe*)

Cowper, William 160

Cults 52, 124–29

Curtin, Jeremiah (Tr.) 52, 264

Daisy Miller 91–95

Davidson, Angus (Tr.) 252

Decline and Fall of the Roman Empire 125–26

DICKENS, CHARLES **65–68**, **206–08**, **213–15**, 272

Domus Aurea 78, 79, 114

Doney's 200

ELIOT, GEORGE 34, **35–37**, 273

ERASMUS 141, 142–43, **144–49**, 273

EVELYN, JOHN **55–57**, 57–58, 274

Feasting 71–77

Fever 88, 95, 195

Finley, M.I. (Tr.) 228

Fleeting Rome 45

Footsteps, Adventures of a Romantic Biographer 182–83

Forum 13, **48–52**, 229, 237, 245

Fountains 18 (*see also Piazza Navona; Trevi Fountain*)

Frontinus, Sextus Julius 249

Garibaldi, Giuseppe 153

Ghetto 53–61

GIBBON, EDWARD 7, **13**, 102, **125–26**, 274

Gide, André 11

GISSING, GEORGE **264–65**, 275

GOETHE 31, 32, **33–34**, 168–69, **169–70**, 275

Golden Ass, The 126–29

Goldsmith, Oliver 41–42

Grand Hotel 223ff

GRAVES, ROBERT **237–40**, 276

GRAY, THOMAS 12, **12–13**, **138–40**, 160, 276

GREGOROVIUS, FERDINAND **109–11**, **136**, 137, **142–43**, 276

Hadrian the Seventh 131–35

Hadrian, emperor 210

Hamilton, Gavin 10

Hamilton, Mrs G.W. (Tr.) 111, 136, 143

HARDY, THOMAS **194–95**, 277

HARE, AUGUSTUS 7, **180–82**, 277

HAWTHORNE, NATHANIEL, **103–05**, 171, **187**, 195, 200, **201–03**, **252–54**, 266, 277, 290

HAZLITT, WILLIAM **15–16**, **58–59**, 171, 184, 278

History of the City of Rome in the Middle Ages 109–11, 136, 142–43

HOBHOUSE, JOHN CAM **122–24**, 278

HOLMES, RICHARD **182–83**, 278

HORACE **242**, 279

HOUGHTON, LORD **217–23**, 278

House of Life, The 251–52

Howells, W.D. 47

Howitt, Mary (Tr.) 205

HUTTON, EDWARD **64–65**, 279

Hymn to Proserpine 107–08

I, Claudius 237–40

Ides of March, The 97–98

Improvisatore, The 203–05

INGRES **177**, 279

Italian Hours 187–88

Italian Journey 170

JAMES, HENRY 25–26, **26–28**, **29–31**, 65, **91–95**, 164, **165–66**, **187–88**, 195, 280, 290

Jews of Rome 53ff, 85, 96

JOHNSON, ROBERT UNDERWOOD **266**, 280

Joyce, James 192

Jugurtha 106

Julia, daughter of Augustus 231, 232, 239

Julius Caesar 97

Julius Exclusus 144–49

Julius II, pope 141, 144–49

Jung, Carl 11

Juno Moneta, temple of 102

JUVENAL 20, **20–23**,

KEATS, JOHN 217–23, **218–19**, 281

Keats, house of 217ff, 223, 281

L'Improvisatore 63, 203–05

Livy 96

LAHIRI, JHUMPA **59–61**, 281

LEAR, EDWARD **163–64**, 281–82

Leo X, pope 109ff, 141

Leo XII, pope 177

Leonardo da Vinci 186

LEVI, CARLO **43–45**, 282

Ludovisi Juno 168, 170

Luther, Martin 141

Macaulay, Thomas Babington 137, 167

MACINNES, HELEN **199–200**, 282

Mamertine Prison 102–05

Marble Faun, The 200, 201–03, 252–54

Marble, Joan 249

Marcus Aurelius, equestrian statue of 188ff

MARTIAL **79**, **80**, 282

Medwin, Thomas 160

Melville, Herman 160, 161

Messalina 247–48

Michelangelo 12, 137, 168, 184–87, 188

Middlemarch 35–37

MILTON, JOHN **116–20**, 283

Mirabilia Urbis Romae 97–98, 99–102

MONTAIGNE, MICHEL DE **134–35**, 283

MORRITT, J.B.S. **84**, 137, 283

MUNTHE, AXEL 223, **224–27**, 284

Nero, emperor 49, 74, 75, 78, 85, 259, 285, 286, 289; (fire of) 111ff

New York Times, The 19–20, 68–70, 131

Nicholas V, pope 141

Nichols, E.M. (Tr.) 102

North from Rome 199–200

Octavian (*see* Augustus)

On Heroes and Hero-Worship 141–42

Oppian Law 228, 229

OUIDA **161–63**, 284

OVID 235, **236**, 285

Palatine Hill 183, 194, 247

Palazzo Ricci (Via Giulia) 252

Paradise Regained 117–20

Passionate Sightseer, The 183–84

PATOUN, WILLIAM **8–10**, 42, 285

Paul IV, pope 53

Paul, St 111

Peter, St 103, 104, 105, 111, 144–49

PETRONIUS ARBITER 49, 52, 74, **75–77**, 258, 259ff, 285–86

Phillimore, J.S. (Tr.) 235, 244

Piazza del Popolo 12–13, 68, 158

Piazza di Spagna 8, 10, 25, 64, 158

Piazza Navona 18, 251

Pictures from Italy 65–68, 206–08, 213–15

Pilate, Pontius 115, 136

Pincian Hill 130, 155, 163–64

Pius IX, pope 131, 276

POE, EDGAR ALLAN **215–17**, 286

Poet's Bazaar, A 149–50

Pomponazzo, Pietro 110–11

Porta del Popolo 12

PORTER, PETER **208–09**, 286

PRAZ, MARIO **251–52**, 286

Promenades dans Rome 87–88

PROPERTIUS 232, **233–35**, 243, **243–44**, 245, 287

Protestant Cemetery 195, 221, 289, 290

Pym, Barbara **140**, 287
QUEVEDO, FRANCISCO DE
  192–93, 287
Quo Vadis 49–52, 259–64
Ramsay, G.G. (Tr.) 23
Raphael 37, 171, 177, 204, 205
Reformation 140ff
Reni, Guido 171, 211
Richter, Jean-Paul (Tr.) 187
Ring and the Book, The 211–13
Roba di Roma 62–64, 196–98
Roderick Hudson 26–31,
  165–66
ROLFE, FREDERICK **131–34**,
  287–88
Roman Elegies 33–34
Roman Fever 88–91
*Rome '44: The Battle for the
  Eternal City* 156–59
RUSKIN, JOHN 42, 137, **138**,
  193–94, 288
S. Giovanni in Porta Latina 55
S. Gregorio della Divina Pietà
  58
S. Lorenzo in Lucina 210, 211
S. Maria della Concezione
  199–205
S. Maria in Aracoeli 101, 102

Santissimo Bambino 102,
  103–05
Scipios, family of 232, 271
Scott, Sir Walter 10, 284
SENECA **71–72**, 79, 255,
  255–56, 288–89
Severn, Joseph 217, 218–20,
  222, 223
SHELLEY, PERCY BYSSHE 12, **14**,
  15, 47, **83**, 105, **106**, 137,
  183, **185–86**, 221, **222–23**,
  240, **240–41**, **250–51**, 255,
  270, 272, 289
Shugaar, Antony (Tr.) 45
Sibyl, Tiburtine 101
SIENKIEWICZ, HENRYK **49–52**,
  74–75, **259–64**, 289
Sigeric of Glastonbury 99
Sistine Chapel 183–84, 185,
  187
Sitwell, Sacheverell 171
Smithers, Leonard (Tr.) 243
SMOLLETT, TOBIAS **17–19**, **84–
  85**, **167–68**, **250**, **256–58**,
  289–90
Solace of Pilgrimes, Ye 189–91
Spanish Steps 62–65, 218
Spender, Stephen 84

St Peter's 13, 15, 24, 25, 29–31,
   132, 134, 135–40, 155, 159
STAËL, MADAME DE 37–38,
   38–41, 274, 290
Stark, Dame Freya 249
STENDHAL 83–84, **87–88**, 290
Story of San Michele, The
   224–27
STORY, WILLIAM WETMORE
   62–64, 195, **196–98**, 290
Strachey, Lytton 14
SWINBURNE, ALGERNON CHARLES
   106, **107–08**, 291
Symonds, John Addington (Tr.)
   153, 180
TACITUS **112–16**, 286, 292
Tarpeian Rock 17, 201
Tiberius, emperor 115, 116,
   118, 136
Time in Rome, A 47–48, 245–48
Titus, emperor 81, 82, 85, 88
Trajan's Column 100
Travels through France and Italy
   17–19, 84–85, 167–68, 250,
   256–58
TREVELYAN, RALEIGH **156–59**,
   292
Trevi Fountain 251, 266

Trimalchio 74, 75–77
TWAIN, MARK 171, **172–76**,
   292–93
Unaccustomed Earth 59–61
VARRO **72**, 293
Vatican 130ff, 181
Veranilda 264–65
Veronica, St 136
Vespasian, emperor 85
Vestal Virgins 245–48
Via Appia 206, 208
Via del Babuino 8, 163
Via Giulia 251–52
Via Vittorio Veneto 199
Villa Farnesina 37
Villa Giulia 60
Vitellius, emperor 71, 75
Volusian 136
Walks in Rome 7, 180–82
Walpole, Sir Horace 12, 14,
   160
WHARTON, EDITH **88–91**,
   293–94
WILDER, THORNTON **97–98**, 294
William Wilson 215–17
Woolf, Virginia 11
WORDSWORTH, WILLIAM 16, **17**,
   137, 294

INDEX OF SIGHTS

Extracted from the General Index, for easy reference, a list of the sights, streets, works of art and artists mentioned by the authors quoted in this literary companion:

Apollo Belvedere, statue 167, 269

Baths of Caracalla 183, 254, 255

Baths of Diocletian 254

Borghese Gallery 171

Borghese Gardens 43–45

Caffè Greco 62, 163

Campo de' Fiori 59

Capitoline Hill 17, 38, 100, 187–88, 274

Capitoline Venus, statue 167, 177

Capuchin church 199–205

Castel Sant'Angelo 150, 151–53

Catacombs 205–08

Cestius, Pyramid of 34, 221

Colosseum 78–95

Constantine, Arch of 105–06

Corso 65, 67, 68, 70, 158, 165, 187

Domus Aurea 78, 79, 114

Doney's 200

Forum 13, 48–52, 229, 237, 245

Ghetto 53–61

Goethe, museum 169

Grand Hotel 223ff

Juno Moneta, temple of 102

Keats, house of 217ff, 223, 281

Ludovisi Juno 168, 170

Mamertine Prison 103–05

Marcus Aurelius, equestrian statue of 188ff

Michelangelo 12, 137, 184–87, 188; (*Last Judgement*) 185–86, 187; (*Moses*) 168, 185; (*Risen Christ*) 168

Palatine Hill 183, 194, 247

Palazzo Altemps 170

Palazzo Ricci (Via Giulia) 252

Piazza del Popolo 12–13, 68, 158

Piazza di Spagna 8, 10, 25, 64, 158

Piazza Navona 18, 251

Pincian Hill 130, 155, 163–64

Porta del Popolo 12

Praz, Mario, museum 287

Protestant Cemetery 195, 221, 289, 290

Raphael 37, 171, 177, 204, 205

Reni, Guido 171, 211

S. Giovanni in Porta Latina 55

S. Gregorio della Divina Pietà 58

S. Lorenzo in Lucina 210, 211

S. Maria in Aracoeli 101, 102

S. Maria della Concezione 199–205

S. Maria sopra Minerva 168

S. Pietro in Vincoli 168

Scipios, tomb of 232

Sistine Chapel 183–84, 185, 187

Spanish Steps 62–65, 218

St Peter's 13, 15, 24, 25, 29–31, 132, 134, 135–40, 155, 159

Tarpeian Rock 17, 201

Trajan's Column 100

Trevi Fountain 251, 266

Vatican 130ff, 181

Vestal Virgins (atrium of) 245, 247; (temple of) 245

Via Appia 206, 208

Via del Babuino 8, 163

Via Giulia 251–52

Via Vittorio Veneto 199

Villa Farnesina 37

Villa Giulia 60

ACKNOWLEDGEMENTS

Every effort has been made to contact the copyright holders of material used. We would be pleased to hear from any copyright owners we have been unable to reach to ensure that proper redress is made and that due accreditation is given in future editions. Thanks are due to all authors and publishers who granted permission to reproduce extracts as follows:

Thames & Hudson for *The Passionate Sightseer* by Bernard Berenson, 1960; The estate of Axel Munthe for *The Story of San Michele*, © 1929; John Murray for *A Traveller's Prelude* by Freya Stark, 1950; Pan Macmillan for *A Very Private Eye* by Barbara Pym, 1984; The estate of Helen MacInnes for *North from Rome* © 1958; Bloomsbury Publishing Plc for *Unaccustomed Earth* by Jhumpa Lahiri © 2008, and used by permission of Alfred A. Knopf, a division of Random House, Inc.; John Wiley & Sons Ltd for *Fleeting Rome: In Search of La Dolce Vita* by Carlo Levi © 2004; Carcanet Press Limited for *I, Claudius* by Robert Graves (1974 Penguin edition). Extract from *Rome '44: The Battle for the Eternal City*, © Raleigh Trevelyan 1981, reprinted by permission of A.M. Heath & Co Ltd.; Extract from *A Time in Rome* reproduced with permission of Curtis Brown Group Ltd, London, on behalf of the estate of Elizabeth Bowen, © Elizabeth Bowen 1959. *The Pines of Rome* © Peter Porter, 1999; *The Ides of March* copyright © 1948 by Wilder Family LLC. Reprinted by arrangement with The Wilder Family LLC and The Barbara Hogenson Agency, Inc. All rights reserved; *Footsteps: Adventures of a Romantic Biographer* published by Hodder & Stoughton, 1985; Extract from 'Roman Fever' reprinted with the permission of Scribner, a division of Simon & Schuster, Inc., from *Roman Fever and Other Stories* by Edith Wharton, copyright © 1934 by Liberty Magazine, copyright renewed © 1962 by William R. Tyler. All rights reserved. Also by permission of the Edith Wharton Estate and the Watkins/Loomis Agency. Excerpt by Sacheverell Sitwell from *Grand Tour: A Journey in the Tracks of the Age of Aristocracy* (© Sacheverell Sitwell, 1935) is reproduced by permission of PFD (www.pfd.co.uk) on behalf of the Estate of Sacheverell Sitwell.

Images: Wikicommons: pp. 267, 268, 282, 283, 284; © 2010 Jupiterimages Corporation: pp. 6, 269 (top), 271, 273, 274 (top), 277 (top), 278, 280, 281, 289; The University of Texas at Austin: pp. 269 (below), 272, 274 (below), 275, 290, 294; The Library of Congress: pp. 277 (below), 286, 291, 292, 293.